Overcoming ADHD

Overcoming ADHD

Helping Your Child Become Calm,
Engaged, and Focused—Without a Pill

STANLEY I. GREENSPAN, M.D.

With Jacob Greenspan

A Merloyd Lawrence Book

Da Capo Press • Lifelong Books
A Member of the Perseus Books Group

616.8589
GRE

Designed by Jeff Williams
Set in Adobe Garamond by the Perseus Books Group

Library of Congress Cataloging-in-Publication Data
Greenspan, Stanley I.
   Overcoming ADHD : helping your child become calm, engaged, and focused—without a pill / Stanley I. Greenspan ; with Jacob Greenspan.—1st Da Capo Press ed.
      p. cm.
   Includes bibliographical references and index.
   ISBN 978-0-7382-1355-2 (alk. paper)
   1. Attention-deficit hyperactivity disorder. 2. Behavior modification. I. Greenspan, Jacob. II. Title.

RJ506.H9G75 2009
618.92'8589—dc22

2009013098

First Da Capo Press edition 2009

Published as a Merloyd Lawrence Book by Da Capo Press
A Member of the Perseus Books Group
www.dacapopress.com

Note: The information in this book is true and complete to the best of our knowledge. This book is intended only as an informative guide for those wishing to know more about health issues. In no way is this book intended to replace, countermand, or conflict with the advice given to you by your own physician. The ultimate decision concerning care should be made between you and your doctor. We strongly recommend you follow his or her advice. Information in this book is general and is offered with no guarantees on the part of the authors or Da Capo Press. The authors and publisher disclaim all liability in connection with the use of this book. The names and identifying details of people associated with events described in this book have been changed. Any similarity to actual persons is coincidental.

Da Capo Press books are available at special discounts for bulk purchases in the U.S. by corporations, institutions, and other organizations. For more information, please contact the Special Markets Department at the Perseus Books Group, 2300 Chestnut Street, Suite 200, Philadelphia, PA, 19103, or call (800) 810-4145, ext. 5000, or e-mail special.markets@perseusbooks.com.

10 9 8 7 6 5 4 3 2 1

To Andy

Contents

Acknowledgments

I want to thank all the children and families with whom I have the honor of working to develop the approach outlined in this book. I also want to thank my family for their support, Sarah Miller for working with the families so effectively, Sue Morrisson for her administrative support, Jill Newman for her overall office support, and especially Merloyd Lawrence for her usual extraordinary editing and guidance in bringing this book to fruition.

CHAPTER 1

A New Way of Looking at ADHD and ADD

Millions of children, as well as a large number of adults, are diagnosed with attention deficit and hyperactivity disorders. Although estimates vary from 1 percent to 20 percent, most researchers believe that approximately 8 percent or more of children have this disorder. Today, the vast majority of these children and adults are put on medication as the main feature of their treatment. Some children may also receive special accommodation at school, such as sitting in the front row, and they may participate in many types of behavior management programs to limit impulsive or inappropriate behavior. Unfortunately, such programs rarely address the underlying reasons for a child's difficulties with paying attention, focus, and self-control.

Can children and adults with attention deficit disorder (ADD) and attention deficit/hyperactivity disorder

(ADHD) overcome these difficulties without pills? The answer is absolutely yes for the vast majority. The key lies in identifying and treating the problems that underlie each child's or adult's inattentiveness. Many parts of the mind and brain contribute to attention. Each individual has his or her own unique profile. Over the past thirty-five years of clinical practice, I have worked with all age groups affected by ADHD and related disorders—from infants, toddlers, and preschoolers to grade schoolers, adolescents, and adults—as well as conducted many research studies. This experience has made it possible to create a program that systematically strengthens the different abilities that contribute to paying attention and enable each of us to regulate ourselves, to focus on problems to be solved, and to follow through.

From this work, my colleagues and I have developed a new way to think about ADHD. It is not a single disorder like strep throat. Contrary to many current beliefs, it does not involve just one part of the brain or mind. Rather, there are many different roads that lead to the symptoms that we call attention deficit disorders and hyperactivity. For example, because some children are overly reactive to sights, sounds, and other sensations, they become highly distractible. Other children are just the opposite. They crave new sights and sounds as well as touch and, therefore, are constantly on the move, going from one thing to another. Still others are so underreactive to sights, sounds, and sensations in general that they withdraw into their imaginations and, for this reason, appear inattentive. Still other children get "lost in the trees" and have difficulty with visualizing the big picture. Planning and sequencing motor actions are yet another problem area for many children with attentional difficulties.

The ways in which these and other patterns characterize a particular child are at the heart of this new way of thinking about ADHD and ADD. They are also at the heart of the intervention program we have created that tailors the approach to each child and family. Intervention is based on understanding not only the nature of the child's problem with attending and the challenges that develop in daily life and school as a consequence, from infancy through childhood and adolescence, but, more important, how the healthy abilities that make focus and attention possible can be encouraged and strengthened. The motor and cognitive exercises and activities we have developed can strengthen the mind, and there is mounting evidence that when we strengthen the mind we also strengthen the physical structure and functioning of the brain as well. Unfortunately, at present the roots of attention disorders are rarely fully addressed. Treatments focus only on reducing the outward signs of the disorder.

The Nature of Attention

There are two ways to think about attention. One is that it's a feature of the human nervous system, and either you can pay attention or you can't, and if you can't, you need one of the stimulant medications such as Ritalin or

Adderall or Concerta. The other way to think about attention is that it's a learned process with many components. When a baby in the first months of life turns toward Mommy's voice or looks at Daddy's face and gives a big smile, that's the beginning of attention. When a toddler takes Mommy by the hand to the toy shelf and points up to the bear she wants, that's an active, practical, problem-solving use of attention. When a child is sitting in the classroom listening to the teacher and following her instructions and then raises his hand to ask for an explanation, that's again a very active, dynamic, problem-solving use of attention.

Variations in attention can be expected in early development. As early as two to four months of age, when babies become more capable of turning and focusing to look at Mother's smiling face and listen and coo responsively to Father's happy voice, they can differ in their ability to sustain attention. At eight to twelve months, some may attend only fleetingly rather than in a sustained manner in back-and-forth games such as peek-a-boo or pat-a-cake or when enjoying a shape-sorter game with a parent. A two year old might just move from toy to toy and appear highly distracted even when playing with a favorite doll or truck. Later, a young child may always be on the move, always changing "topics," unable to stick with a conversation or a game. Another pattern of inattention involves spurts of attention and then inattention or intermittent stop-and-go interactions. Some children may focus on favorite toys or one-way forms of entertainment

(TV, video games, and so on) but find it hard to shift their attention to people, even when their mother or father is calling them.

Sometimes variations in attention can be related to differing motivation, as when young children may be attentive to books, construction sets, or individual projects but less so when they are expected to attend and participate more actively in activities others choose or when there are ground rules, as in "circle time" at school. Often, the tolerance or expectations of those around them affect whether attention is seen as a problem. For example, a child playing alone for long periods might be considered "independent" and "well behaved" rather than self-absorbed. Adults may think it necessary to change activities every few minutes at preschool or at home because they assume that the attention span is very short in young children.

The way that I and many of my colleagues who work with children prefer to think about attention is that it's a dynamic, active process involving many parts of the nervous system at the same time. Attention involves taking in sights and sounds and touch; it involves processing information; it involves planning and executing actions. If you can take in information, process and comprehend it, and plan and execute actions based on this information, you can pretty well pay attention. It's not just about sitting still; there are many gifted people who are very active— they're moving around or fidgeting all the time—yet are very successful professors or engineers or doctors or lawyers or chefs and wonderful parents. What determines whether they're what I would call "functionally attentive" (i.e., taking in and mastering their environment) is how well they get all the different abilities just mentioned working smoothly together. When they are, a person is attentive.

If we think about attention that way, it helps explain the variety of problems that I see in my practice. Of the children who come to see me having been diagnosed with ADD or ADHD, a great majority have what we call "motor planning and sequencing" problems. Almost all of them have difficulties with carrying out a many-step action plan in response to either a verbal request or visual information or an implicit demand of the environment, like solving an obstacle course. Other children—not all of them, but some of them—are overreactive to things like touch or sound, so they get overwhelmed and very easily distracted, for example, by another child sitting next to them at school who's making noise. Their overresponsiveness leads them to be less attentive.

Children who are underresponsive or underreactive to sensation—for whom a normal speaking voice won't register or who won't feel you touching them unless you use firm pressure—are also going to appear inattentive. For example, a little boy came to my office the other day, and I talked to him for a good five minutes in a normal tone of voice before he finally looked up from his electronic game and noticed me. I let it go on for a while because I wanted to see how much he could tune out and how underreactive he was. I learned during the session with him that, when I increased the energy in my voice, I could get his attention within a second every time, but if I talked to him in a normal tone of voice, he basically tuned me out. When we went through his history very carefully, it turned out that he was underreactive in a number of his senses.

Sensory-seeking children may or may not be under-reactive but are constantly looking for more touch, more sight, more sound, more movement, and so they're going to be very active, distractible, and inattentive—they are the typical children who get diagnosed with ADHD.

Other children diagnosed with ADHD may have a problem with processing and sequencing information. If you say, "I need you to go upstairs, put on your shoes, come back down, and get ready to go outside because we're going out to lunch," he may be able to process only the first part of that sequence—"I need you to go upstairs"—and then he forgets what he's supposed to do. His problem with sequencing information makes it difficult for him to hold on to complex verbal instructions. He's going to seem very inattentive because on the way to his room he gets so distracted by a toy that he forgets why he went up in the first place.

The ability to plan and sequence actions and solve problems is commonly referred to as "executive functioning." It's related to motor planning and sequencing and also to sequencing and problem solving with ideas. A good way to think about executive functioning is that it's the child's ability to take in information through the senses, process that information, and then use that information in a sequence of actions to solve a problem. We notice the last part of executive functioning—the planning and sequencing actions or words—but it depends on the first two steps, as well.

Other problems, such as in visual-spatial processing, can play a part in attention. A child who can't see the big picture goes upstairs to find her shoes but doesn't know how to look systematically because she doesn't have a picture of her room. So she goes and looks near the bed, doesn't see them, and then gets distracted because she doesn't have a mental picture of other places the shoes might be.

From these examples we see that a diagnosis of ADD or ADHD may not be simple at all. The inattention is the outward symptom, but the problem is rooted in these deeper elements, like motor planning and sequencing, overreaction, and visual-spatial difficulties.

Cultural Expectations

There are different theories about the causes of ADHD/ADD. Some who study the condition have recently claimed that it is simply a normal difference among individuals and may have conferred an evolutionary advantage on individuals who needed to be very active and reactive in their environments. Obviously, being in a classroom where you need to sit at a desk, focus on the teacher, take in everything she is saying, and think about it can be a difficult task if you are a person who notices everything and wants to get up every few minutes and walk around and discover things. Since many more boys are diagnosed with ADHD than girls, this difference has been attributed to our long evolutionary history, that is, men were expected to go out and hunt in a dangerous environment to provide the daily food for the family. In today's industrialized society, there is less and less emphasis on outdoor activities and higher expectations for sitting and focusing and paying attention in a classroom or office. Even recreation or playtime seems to be more passive now—sitting in front of a computer screen and playing video games, for example. Clearly, cultural expectations and opportunities need to be taken into account in the definition of ADHD. As we will discuss more fully later, one of the goals of this book is to help children deal flexibly and appropriately with the demands of different environments, such as being very active and alert to all signals but organized, during sports, dance, or wilderness camping, and more narrowly focused and still when listening to a teacher give a lecture or instructions.

There are also strong views among many that the causes of ADHD involve specific biological pathways. Neuroscience research currently suggests that the frontal lobes of the brain are involved in ADHD—particularly the prefrontal cortex—and that fundamental difficulties in many of the executive functions (for example, sequencing and planning) are, in a sense, "housed" in the prefrontal cortex and the frontal lobes. Other researchers suggest the cerebellum is involved as well. Such research is ongoing. Whatever direction it takes, children with this diagnosis will benefit from a careful analysis of their particular profiles and attention to the strengths and weaknesses that underlie their hyperactivity or inattention. In the chapters that follow, we've outlined the ways to put together such a program.

CHAPTER 2

A Comprehensive Approach

The program that we are going to describe for ADHD and ADD and all other kinds of attention problems, including ones that may not even fit the full criteria for ADHD or ADD, will focus on strengthening each of the separate abilities that support attention, focus, and concentration. This approach doesn't require medication. There is a subgroup of children and adults who benefit from medication, but there is much that can be done before medication is considered. I always do a six- to twelve-month trial of a comprehensive approach in my practice before considering a referral to a psychopharmacology expert for a medication consultation, and I would suggest that this trial is the most important first step. It doesn't rule out the use of medication, but by implementing a comprehensive approach to ADHD and ADD, it becomes clear that there are a lot of children who don't require a "pill" at all. If medication is indicated at some point as part of our comprehensive approach, it's likely to be a lesser dose and of a lesser duration. If we are able to strengthen some of the abilities related to attention but the child still has some difficulties, then medication at a lesser dose and for a shorter period of time may prove helpful until these other abilities become strong enough for the child to maintain full focus and attention.

One of my concerns regarding the use of medication, in addition to the well-known potential side effects, such as agitation, sleep problems, or weight gain, is that many children experience a constriction in their emotional range, in their perceptions. Their creativity or sense of humor may not be as great. Although they can focus more, the medication narrows their horizons. This isn't to say that some children won't still require medication—some will. However, as a general rule I recommend working on strengthening the underlying core issues for at least six to twelve months and seeing how much progress we make before considering medication. If we are beginning to make progress in the first six months in these core issues and we see a better ability to attend and focus, then we have a child whose development is proceeding in a healthier fashion.

Seven Key Goals

In the following chapters, we will discuss each of the elements of a comprehensive intervention approach to ADD and ADHD in greater detail. Below is a brief overview.

1. Strengthening Motor Functioning. Here we work on the child's fundamental ability to use his nervous system and control his body in a healthy, age-appropriate way. This would include balancing, coordination, movement, integrating left and right body parts, hand-eye coordination, fine and gross motor skills, and the like.

2. Helping the Child Plan and Sequence Actions and Thoughts. As I mentioned earlier, almost all children with attention problems have difficulties in sequencing. It's hard for these children to play a treasure-hunt game with a series of clues or to negotiate an obstacle course that involves sequencing many motor actions in a row. Later, they may not be able to follow complex directions in writing an essay. What we call motor planning and sequencing, and sequencing in general, involves verbal sequencing, too, as well as responding to visual cues and visual sequencing.

3. Modulating a Child's Response to Sensations. Many children with ADHD or ADD have challenges in the way they process sensations. Some are sensory craving, while others are sensory overreactive—at least in one or another modality—and are constantly distracted by the stimuli in their environment. Some children may be overreactive to the movement of their own bodies so that moving in space on a swing may overstimulate them, or they may require a lot of jumping, spinning, swinging, and dancing. So this goal involves working with children's unique profiles, helping them find adaptive ways to respond to sensation and stay calm and focused.

4. Reflective Thinking. The fourth goal involves helping children progress up the developmental ladder in terms of their ability to think. We help a child progress from thinking with actions all the way to reflective thinking. A reflective thinker can say, "Gee, this task is hard for me. I had better give myself some reminders." Reflective thinking allows people to know their own strengths and weaknesses and to plan ahead accordingly. This ability enables concentration, focus, and attention in all tasks of home and school.

5. Building Self-Confidence. For many who have felt helpless to control their attention and activity level, anxiety can cause them to be even more distractible and forgetful. When anxious about an assignment or homework, it's easy to play ostrich. As one child told me, "I just put it out of my mind and don't think about it; I just think about the tree outside. I think about what I'm doing now. I don't think about tomorrow. I don't think about the test." Problems in following instructions and paying attention can make a child feel guilty and incompetent, and any comprehensive approach must help a child feel effective and in control.

6. Improving Family Dynamics. Family dynamics play a large role, certainly in emotional coping, but also in the way we master each of these other abilities. Take, for example, reflective thinking: When a child is three or four years old and says, "Mommy, I want to go out," and Mommy says yes or no, it doesn't encourage thinking. But if Mommy or Daddy says, "Why do you want to go out?" all of a sudden the child has to give a logical answer. She might say, "Because I want to play." "Well, why do you want to play outside rather than inside?" "Because the slide is outside." Some families do this naturally, and some don't. So the family component will be important here.

How well we sequence is also a function of family dynamics. The availability of Mom or Dad to be taken by the hand to the refrigerator or work with a child to set up an elaborate train set supports the ability to sequence and focus for longer periods of time. For a child, even a toddler, who is easily distractible, getting even more practice at sequencing and focus will help her learn to attend more effectively. The family dynamics, the patience of the parents, and the way they interact with their children can therefore play a significant role in a child's learning how to pay attention.

7. A Healthy Environment. The physical environment of the child is also critical. For example, for a child who is overreactive, an environment with a lot of noise and commotion is likely to lead to overload and a lot of distractibility. Also, we are discovering that toxic substances, not just lead, which is a well known toxin, but others

called endocrine disrupters, along with still other substances that impair the functioning of the nervous system, can be in the diet and physical environment. This
may include, for example, the impact of paint fumes or
other products a child may either eat or breathe, which
can cause more irritability or distractibility.

The Role of Parents and Caregivers

In later chapters, we will give examples of how parents
and caregivers can help in each of these seven parts of a
comprehensive approach. Here, we would like to men-
tion a few general ways in which adults and children interact that can be significant contributors to attentional
challenges, and how to make them more positive.

Some infants and children seem to communicate only
in short, telegraphic bursts rather than in long chains of
back-and-forth signaling. Some caregivers respond to
these short, unrelated communications by becoming as
fragmented as the child. They jump from one thing to
another with the child rather than trying to sustain a long
chain of interaction. Some become frustrated and just let
the child play alone.

Other caregivers attempt to overcontrol the child,
which can lead the child to become rigid. Such a child
seems to focus, but it is not true, shared attention. There
is no spontaneous dialogue, no real engagement on the
part of the child. Forcing attention may lead to outbursts
of anger or defiance that end any joint activities. Both a

child's natural developmental differences and a caregiver's characteristics (including attentional difficulties in caregivers themselves) can contribute to this type of pattern. The absence of consistent opportunities for communication and interaction with adults can lead children to become more self-absorbed or preoccupied with their own interests and seemingly inattentive to others. These same children, however, can be readily wooed into interaction and focus when engaged in a quiet environment, in a small group, with a patient parent or teacher. As we said earlier, what appears to be poor attention may also be related to anxiety and avoidance patterns. Chaotic families or harsh or judgmental ones can certainly contribute, and children can withdraw and seem depressed.

When a family and caregivers are giving the children many opportunities for regulation, interaction, and engagement, poor attention in children is then usually related to one or more underlying difficulties in processing sensations, in motor planning and sequencing, in thinking skills, and in the child's physical environment. Each of these is discussed in the following chapters.

In working to strengthen each of these areas, certain general principles are useful. First of all, in playing with a child or engaging in a joint activity, the key is to *join the child in his rhythm*. If he is more active, try to move with him. If he is slower moving and seems to be more absentminded, get into a slow-moving rhythm with him.

It is also very important to *pay attention to the child's natural preferences* and harness his enthusiasm. Does he enjoy vigorous movement or sitting still? Does he enjoy one toy versus another? If he prefers his toys over a person, you can engage him with these toys—for example, place the toy on your head or hide it and create a problem for the child to solve. By doing that, he is drawn into interaction. The caregiver and the toy become one and the same. Once the child is motivated and you are in rhythm together, the key is to extend your interaction. Add new twists to the game.

It is important *not to get caught up in repetitive actions* (i.e., opening and closing a door or putting a toy car in and out of a garage). Try to move to more creative and innovative actions to sustain the child's attention and focus.

Another key to helping a child with sensory processing difficulties is to *find the right level of sensation.* If the child is overresponsive, you have to be soothing. If the child is underresponsive, you have to energize up in an animated and interesting way. This can be done for each of the child's senses. For example, for a child who is overresponsive to sound, use soothing vocalizations. If a child is underresponsive to sound, use highly energized vocalizations. Find out whether he responds better to high- or low-pitched sounds. For a child who is easily overloaded by visual complexity, keep the visual challenge simple. For a child who requires visual complexity, a lot of colors and patterns is preferable. A child who prefers robust movement in space may enjoy roughhousing or other gymnastics. A child who is initially more stationary has to be approached more gradually and enticed into greater movement. For the child who has trouble with auditory processing, start with simple vocalizations or words, building up to more complicated ones, including, as the child gets older, games that the child can win by following gradually more complex directions.

In all these activities, the child is learning to attend, interact, and use his senses more adaptively, at the same time. As you tune in to the child's rhythms, find what pleases him, join those pleasurable activities, extend circles of communication, and harness all the sensory processing and motor planning abilities of the child simultaneously, you are strengthening his underlying processing capacities as well as helping that child learn to focus and attend.

As part of this comprehensive approach, many children require specific therapeutic or educational therapies. For example, some children may require occupational or speech therapy. Ideally, such programs are begun during the toddler years during the stage at which the child is just learning how to sustain attention and engage in shared social problem solving. By using the techniques of occupational and speech therapies, the child can be helped to become a dynamic attender and a problem solver. Even for older children, such programs can be helpful.

Modulating Hyperactivity

Not infrequently, children with attentional problems also have difficulty controlling their activity level. Thus, the most common label is ADHD rather than ADD. They can become constantly active, intruding into other people's space, or seemingly passive, lost in their own worlds. These patterns are often already in evidence in the infant and toddler. An adult interacting with a small child, however, can modulate the activity. At first the adult can simply join the activity, but then gradually slow it down. With the slightly older child, "modulation games" can be played, such as a copycat game in which each side quickly instructs the other to go fast, slow, or superslow, or play a drum hard, soft, or supersoft. The child who is always shouting and drowning out others with his voice can be helped to modulate his voice by imitating soft sounds and whisper sounds, as well as loud ones.

A parent or other interactive partner may have more influence on a child's level of activity than we are accustomed to assuming. A parent's pattern of response can increase the frequency and intensity of the child's behavior. It can influence the rigidity or emotional sensitivity of the behavior. The more variable or unpredictable a pattern of response (or reinforcement), the less likely it is to help the child adjust or control her behavior. On the other hand, a completely predictable set response is not helpful, either, for it does not help a child become sensitive to changing environments or to the needs of others.

Consider the following examples. A mother is very preoccupied and responds to each of the child's gestures or appeals, but does so in a somewhat unpredictable manner (this is called a random ratio pattern of response or reinforcement). Such a pattern leads to very high activity levels because the more the child does, the more responses (reinforcements) he gets. In contrast, if a parent's response to the child is based on how much time has passed (e.g., a self-absorbed caregiver tunes into the child only periodically), this will lead to less and less activity. Such a pattern where the caregiver responds one time after five seconds and the next time after eight seconds, and so on dampens the child's interest in initiating communication and play. The activity can get so low that the child looks more and more self-absorbed. These patterns of response can exert a potent influence on behavior (Ferster and Skinner 1957). The influence can be subtle, and it may appear that only the child's innate biology is controlling his behavior. Often, however, both biological and experientially based factors are working together (Greenspan 1975).

As you can see, problems with attention can have a number of different developmental pathways. Each of them combines the child's unique "processing" profiles with different types of child-caregiver interaction patterns. In a comprehensive approach, we work on each underlying difficulty (processing, motor planning, and so forth) to build a foundation for engagement and focused attention.

CHAPTER 3

Stephanie

The story of Stephanie, an eight-year-old patient in our practice, illustrates our approach to ADHD and how we help children overcome the challenge of learning to pay attention. Her name and other identifying information have been changed.

Stephanie came to us because she was having difficulty with reading and math in school and because her teacher had labeled her as having ADHD. At school, she was active all the time, chitchatting with her friends and darting about the classroom. At home, Stephanie was also always on the move, getting into frequent conflicts with her sister, even becoming aggressive, which is unusual for a girl her age. Her teacher kept putting pressure on Stephanie's parents to see her as having ADHD and get her "medicated" to improve her focus and attention. Stephanie was in the second grade and heading into the third grade very shortly, and her parents were told she wouldn't be able to keep up with the work, given her "ADHD."

When I initially observed Stephanie in my office, I saw a spirited girl who came in with two motivated, conscientious, thoughtful parents. (Dad was an attorney, and Mom, who previously worked in public relations, stayed at home with Stephanie and her two younger siblings.) Stephanie was indeed active, and her curls bounced as she explored every corner of the office, getting up and down, fidgeting, and moving her arms and legs all the time. Not only was her activity level very high, but her thoughts shifted rapidly as well. When I observed Stephanie with her parents and individually, she would jump from topic to topic, from who was mean to her at school to what's behind the door in my office and then back to her friends and then to how she hated math, and so on. Even when I talked to Stephanie alone, it was hard for her to develop a topic. For example, when I asked her why she thought a certain friend was mean, she would say, "She's mean to everyone" or "I don't think she likes me," but then quickly jump to examine one of the toys and games in my office. When I watched Stephanie's parents with her, they tended to structure things to try to bring her back on topic, but without much success.

I suggested that Stephanie and her parents talk about what they might talk about at home so I could see the flavor of their relationship. Mom said Stephanie occasionally liked to help with cooking, so Mom opened up with "What do you want to help me cook today?"

Stephanie, who loves sweets, smiled at her mother and said, "I want to make my favorite lemon pie."

As we reviewed Stephanie's history, we saw that she had always had difficulties in certain areas ever since she was little. When she was a toddler, she flew about and explored everything. Her parents thought this was a sign of intellectual curiosity and potential. Indeed, Stephanie was a very bright little girl, but had difficulty remaining with an interest for more than a moment. Despite her constant activity, Stephanie showed a warm attachment to her parents and a lively range of feelings and humor in describing her "pesky" siblings.

Now with math in the second grade, Stephanie's problem wasn't in comprehension but in slowing down long enough to understand the methods behind solving the problems. She was very impatient and wanted to speed through things. She tried to finish so quickly that she often made mistakes.

Stephanie was called the family "whirlwind." She liked music and sports, and was an enthusiastic soccer player. She was well coordinated, but frequently didn't follow the rules because she was so eager and couldn't slow down. She had difficulty following directions, whether they were verbal, like giving her three or four clues in a treasure-hunt game or following directions at school, or visual clues, like reading a map with clues to how to find something. Her challenges seemed to be across the board.

Stephanie also showed some sensitivities, being over-reactive to noises, particularly to high-pitched sounds. If music was in the higher frequencies, as in much popular music, she would get more active, move around more, and sometimes hold her ears. She also avoided certain types of touch, like smooth, silky things and foods that were slippery or "slushy."

When we evaluated Stephanie further, we found that even though she was good at sports, fine motor skills were difficult for her. Her handwriting was sloppy and hard to read, and when she took piano lessons she struggled to manage the fingering. She preferred to play the drums because she could pound away and move around more.

In our discussions with Stephanie, we found that she was more of an all-or-nothing thinker rather than one who would look at subtle variations in what she heard or comprehended. In her preferences and friendships, Stephanie tended to go from one extreme to the other—she loves me, she hates me, rather than she likes me a little bit or not too much. This carried over to math concepts—that's tiny, rather than "bigger than this." Stephanie didn't have an internal feel for graduated amounts, whether it was emotions, math, or annoyances from her siblings.

Observing all these facets of a child's profile takes several sessions with both child and parents. In contrast to many approaches to diagnosis, which often consist of a parental or teacher report and session of observation, followed by a prescription, our approach takes in a number of evaluations, often involving more than one professional.

Rather than simply labeling Stephanie as having ADHD, we saw her as a child who had uneven growth in making sense out of different elements of her world and in regulating how she responded to sound, sight, and touch. She also had problems with how she planned her actions and thought.

As we go along further in this book, you will see that we take the position that children do best when we consider them as individuals and understand their unique developmental profile, their strengths and weaknesses, particularly in these core abilities and, most important, to help them get to higher and higher levels of thinking. You will also see some of the methods and exercises we use to strengthen weak areas.

With such efforts we can help children get over the tendency to be sensory seeking or on the move all the time or help them master their overreactivity to certain sights and sounds. We can also help them to plan and sequence their actions more effectively and improve their basic bodily and motor skills—for example, their ability to take notes and write, using fine motor skills. We can help them not only become more coordinated but also carry out complex actions like in a ballet or a dance.

When we look at Stephanie, we have to ask whether Stephanie is characteristic of many children with ADHD. We have just completed a study of children who showed the symptoms of ADHD on all the checklists and met the criteria of ADHD in diagnostic manuals and other research checklist systems. We found that although their symptoms of inattention and high activity were often the same, each one had a slightly different way of taking in sensations, planning actions, sequencing, and so forth. They had different sensory profiles, different levels of thinking, different levels of self-awareness. We found that children with this common set of symptoms showed enormous varieties in the underlying pathways. This raises a question: Do we want to find the underlying causes and strengthen the core abilities, or do we want to focus on only the surface symptoms?

When we look at human beings, we can't look at just one function in isolation because they are all related. We can't look only at attention because it's related to motor development, sensory reactions, thinking, and the role of emotions. We like to use the metaphor of a tree. The roots are the reasons for both healthy development and for the many different symptoms of ADHD, like challenges in the ability to take in what we see and hear, how we plan actions and react to sensations. The tree trunk is our thinking ability, how strong it is and how high it can grow. Then the branches and leaves are the various abilities, like reading, writing, math, science, and the many nonacademic abilities. This model for ADHD works very well. We want to strengthen the roots and the trunk.

Over a period of two years, Stephanie flowered with an approach that provided Stephanie's parents with fun exercises they could do every day that strengthened her core capacities. (These exercises are described in full in

Chapters 4–7.) As Stephanie grew older, she also developed a skill that is vital for children and adults with ADHD. She became more self-aware. She learned to evaluate herself: "I don't need to be in a hurry" or "I'm paying attention better." She learned to reflect on her feelings: "I like Betty better than Harriet because Betty is more like me or our families are alike." In school this kind of reflective thinking was vital: "This wasn't a very good essay" or "I'm having a harder time listening today because of . . ." If a child can learn to see the big picture, the child then has a framework in her mind that helps put problems into perspective. The ability to think reflectively allows children to fill in the pieces even if they don't hear everything the teacher says. This is an ability that is more important than just paying attention.

How many children make the progress we have seen in Stephanie? In my practice, I have found that if the vast majority of parents and schools and children cooperate, and even if it's only the parents and children, we see growth overall in focus and attention.

The remainder of the book will go into the details of how to look at each child as a unique individual and tailor a comprehensive program for that child. You will be able to extrapolate how to apply this program to different children in different situations.

CHAPTER 4

Organizing and Planning
Actions: The Motor System

As we discussed in Chapters 1 and 2, children can have difficulty in paying attention for a wide variety of reasons, from being underreactive to sensations, to craving sensation, to being overreactive, to difficulties processing information and problems planning their actions. Most children with ADHD and ADD have some combination of these problems. A study is currently under way to document the variety of patterns that contribute to this one "common pathway": difficulty in paying attention and hyperactivity. In this chapter, we will examine one of these patterns, involving the motor system.

Weaknesses in motor skills, motor planning, and sequencing are frequently found in children with ADHD. Most require some level of work in each of these three areas. We can work with each child on all these areas simultaneously. The swiftness with which they master the exercises or games or playful activities in each will determine how much work we need to do.

Motor Skills

A child may have trouble with basic motor skills: being able to move left, right, forward, and backward, and doing so with growing dexterity and coordination. To help strengthen these skills for younger children, I like to recommend a series of activities starting with the Evolution Game, with wormlike or snakelike crawling or slithering on the ground, then moving on all fours, then different kinds of balancing on all fours, and then balancing in upright positions. After that we can work on children's ability to coordinate what they see and hear with how they move—left, right, forward, backward, according to different sights and sounds and doing it more quickly. Then we can begin to work on eye-hand coordination and foot-eye coordination, doing it to rhythm and music and with timing exercises. Fantasy play and pretending to be a bird or an action figure can make these games more fun for children. For older children, we can also use the Evolution Game, but sports and dance may be a more enjoyable way for them to learn to master movement patterns.

Motor skills are fundamental to paying attention. You have to have control over your body to be able to focus on any activity. Although some children with low muscle tone are able to concentrate very well and some children who have excellent motor skills might have trouble with concentration, work on these skills generally helps with attention problems. They are a very important foundation piece for general development and help most children learn to attend and focus better.

Games to Improve Motor Skills

Evolution Game

In the "Evolution Game" the idea is to help the child move up the "evolutionary" ladder with progressively more challenging motor activities. All these activities can be accompanied by music or made part of a copycat game. You can stage races or do it in and out and around things to make it more interesting.

- **Slithering.** This starts with slithering movements, like worms or reptiles. You begin by slithering along the ground together with the child. It could be a two-year-old toddler or even a fourteen month old playing copycat with you, or it could be a seven or eight year old slithering with music in the background. Slithering uses all parts of the body— arms, tummy, legs—in a coordinated fashion.

- **Crawling.** From slithering the child moves to crawling on all fours. You can have crawling races and make it more interesting by doing it with music.

- **"Wheelbarrow" Walking.** In "wheelbarrow" walking you hold the child's legs while he walks on his hands. This, too, can be done as a race.

- **Walking.** Then we go to upright walking with nice, coordinated arm movements.

- **Running, Skipping, Hopping, Jumping.** Next, we go to running, skipping, and then hopping—whichever is easier for the child—and then to jumping. It is often easier to start jumping with both legs, then hopping on one leg at a time, and then skipping. Again, adult and child do it together to make it fun.

If the child is able to do some of these activities effortlessly, we can move up the "evolutionary" ladder very quickly. However, if the child has a hard time slithering or a hard time crawling, you can focus on that activity for a while.

- **Agility Drills.** Once we've gone up the ladder, through skipping and hopping and running, then, if the child is interested, we can do some more agility drills, sidestepping left and right, different dance steps, athletic steps, crossing legs over one another—adding variety to make it a little more interesting.

- **Adding Rhythm.** The next step will involve a little more rhythmic activity. We put on some music—some slow, methodical beats, some faster beats—and move rhythmically to the music. We usually do this at the level the child shows the highest level of competency. So if they are running, hopping, and skipping, we can run, hop, and skip in rhythm to the music. If they are just walking, then we will walk to the music and do some dances. But we have to march together or walk together or run together and do it rhythmically to the music.

Modulation Game

After the Evolution Game comes what we call the "Modulation Game" in which we help the child do an activity faster and then slower and then superslow and then super-superslow and then from super-superslow back up to fast—again, at the highest level in which the child can show coordinated action.

The Modulation Game can be a copycat game in which you start with walking or moving, then with clapping hands, playing the drums (which could be the table or a bongo drum), or using our voices (making sounds or singing songs loud, soft, supersoft, back up to loud again). This activity is to help the child learn to regulate and modulate activity in all ways—with hands, legs, whole bodies, coordinated activities, voices, and so forth.

Again, most time is spent on those activities with which the child has the most difficulty. Some will have more difficulty with rhythmic activity or modulation, so you can put a little greater focus on that and use the other activities as just a warm-up. If the child is really competent at the preliminary exercises and seems to be getting bored, you can go right into the midlevel of the Evolution Game or the highest level of the Modulation Game.

Competition and Incentives. When introducing points and rewards for these games, the key is to make the child successful 70 to 80 percent of the time. In a competition, let children beat you 70 to 80 percent of the time so they stay encouraged. If you make it too hard, they will get frustrated and avoid the activity. Don't move on to a higher level until they are successful 70 to 80 percent of the time at the level you are working.

Body Awareness Games

Once the child is comfortable walking, moving, running, and hopping and skipping, the "Body Awareness Game" brings in another facet of motor and sensory functioning:

- **In, Out, Above, Below, and Through.** The child moves in and out, above and below, and through physical objects in relationship to other moving bodies. You can use your hands or some physical structure you've created such as a little platform they have to crawl under or over or a tunnel they have to crawl through.

- **Go Low and High, Go Left and Right.** Then you can add moving hands or other objects (balloons, people, and so on), and the game is to avoid being touched while going through, under, around (left and right), and over objects. In this activity, children gain an awareness of where their bodies begin and where their bodies end.

- **Left and Right Sides of Body.** Next are activities that integrate different parts of the body with sights and sounds: hand-eye, leg-eye, sound-leg, and sound-hand movement patterns. First you can do simple things like throwing a ball with both hands, then with one hand. Play Simon Says games or copycat games in which the child has to touch his left hand to his right shoulder, right hand to left shoulder, right hand to left knee, left hand to right knee and so forth to encourage this awareness. You can vary this in many ways, as long as the child is coordinating the left and right sides of his body, starting off using both hands, then one hand at a time in relation to the other side of the body. You can improvise and make it fun, letting the child win points for doing it right and lose points for doing it wrong. Little prizes for incentives work great with this activity. Again, if the child does this effortlessly, we don't need to spend a lot of time on such left-right types of games.

- **Both Feet and Hands and Different Sides of the Body.** These activities can progress to using both feet and hands and feet and hands on different sides of the body. Exercises can involve the upper part of the body and the lower part, such as bringing hands down to knees, or legs up to waist, and so forth. Such exercises can be found in *Brain Gym: Simple Activities for Whole Brain Learning* (Dennison and Dennison 1992).

- **Coordinating Hand-Eye, Hand-Leg, Sound-Eye, and Sound-Leg.** Then you can move on to more elaborate coordination exercises. Playing catch can involve throwing and catching with both hands, then with the left hand, and then the right hand. Then a child can throw and try to catch the ball herself with her left hand, with her right hand, with both hands. This can be combined with kicking a soft rubber ball or a Nerf ball.

After simply throwing the ball back and forth and making it really easy, then you and the child throw it higher, with both hands, with one hand, the other hand, with both hands, then one hand, then the other hand. Then throw the ball into a basket and then move the basket so that the child has to throw the ball and anticipate where the basket will be as it is moving. Then we have the child first kick the ball to a fixed goal and then to a moving goal. Each time make little games out of it.

After completing the moving-goal game, you can move on to sound-hand and sound-leg exercises in which you keep changing direction for the child—"Kick it left, kick it right." You can have two goals and tell the child to kick it to the right goal and then the left goal, throw it to the basket on the right, throw it to the basket on the left, so it is not just sight and movement but sight, movement, and sound that the child is coordinating. Every time we get more parts of the nervous system working together, we are enhancing the ability to act in a focused way.

Balance and Coordination Games

Next come balance and coordination games. The cerebellum, which is part of the central nervous system at the back of our brains, is responsible for coordination and balance. Balance and coordination are very important factors in focus and attention. However, we don't want to move to these harder balance exercises until the child has mastery of the basics. Again, there will be children who are exceptions to the rule—children who don't do well with balance and coordination but can focus and concentrate very well. These activities and games can help either child—the one who has difficulty in focusing and attending as well as the child who can focus and attend but is weak in balance and coordination.

- **Basic Balance Activities.** Begin with some simple exercises. You can use Koosh pads (round pads, about a foot in diameter, with air foam in them) that you can stand on. (Adults do this to practice their balance and coordination; they also use a balance board where you balance on a board that is resting on a ball and try to keep from falling to one side or the other.) You can also use a balance beam, which could be a piece of wood with enough width for the child's shoe and can be stabilized so it doesn't tip over.

  Start with the child standing on two of these Koosh pads and see if he can balance and for how long. If he can do this effortlessly, have him do it with his eyes closed. Then see if you can increase the time he can do this by a few seconds each day. Then do the same kind of activity standing on one Koosh pad—eyes open, then eyes closed. Then throw a foam ball to the child and have him catch it and throw it back to you while balancing. Then talk to the child and sing songs together while he is balancing with eyes open, then with eyes closed. You can make silly sounds and play copycat games in which the child makes silly sounds with you, with or without music.

- **On One Leg While Doing Other Activities.** Then you can advance up the ladder to doing all the above activities while the child is on one leg—right leg, and then the left leg—while balancing on a Koosh pad. Then do the same with eyes opened, eyes closed, throwing, catching, singing songs, making silly sounds together, or just having a general chitchat.

  You can complicate this even further by having the child catch a ball thrown a little higher so he has a little harder time catching it, while on one leg. The child can throw the ball into a basket while balancing.

- **On a Balance Board.** Once the child has mastered these tasks in balance and coordination using the Koosh pad, you can try the same activities on the balance board (a board resting on a ball). While on the balance board—eyes open, eyes closed, throwing, catching, adding vocalizations—see if the child can throw, catch, and talk all at the same time. If this goes well and the child is a pro at it, you can throw balloons at the child while he tries to avoid the balloons by moving back and forth.

- **On the Balance Beam.** Then you can play some games in which the child is like a gymnast walking on the balance beam but while balloons are coming at him. He has to duck, catch, and throw the balloons while balancing.

All these tasks really improve balance and coordination and can be made a lot of fun for children to do. They build up not just attention and concentration but future dance or athletic skills or current athletic skills because all such activities involve balance and coordination. It is a mistake to assume that children who concentrate easily and focus on schoolwork are not necessarily good at dance, sports, or other activities. These skills should and can go together, although there are exceptions to the rule.

The central goal here is to get many parts of the nervous system working together in a coordinated fashion. This is what really enhances children's ability to regulate and control themselves, and thus to concentrate and focus.

Fine Motor Exercises

As a child develops and gets into the toddler and preschool stages, he is doing more with his fingers and hands, and we want to facilitate that—beyond picking up Cheerios with thumb and forefinger. With a small child, you might ask, "Well, where is that car?" or "Where is that bird?" She may point with her fist or with a finger. If she points with a full fist, that tells us some games that exercise the fine motor system may be needed.

- **Finger Games.** Fine motor games start with little copycat games and rhythmic activities with fingers like playing a make-believe piano or just moving hands and fingers in rhythm. You can go from opening and closing fists and squishing toes to wiggling individual fingers and playing with finger puppets.

- **Coloring and Drawing.** Coloring and drawing are great for fine motor skills and inspire attention. You can start with scribble-scrabble games in which you make a shape and then the child adds something onto the shape and so forth. For example, the child might make a circle and you add eyes and the child adds a little nose and so on, back and forth. Next, the child can do some coloring and eventually copy specific shapes—first lines, then circles, then rectangles, triangles, and diamonds, and then sequences of shapes.

    The goal here is to help children make shapes with lines in all different directions—vertical, horizontal, and connecting the lines together. You can make a bunch of dots and ask the child to connect them together. About 50 percent freelance (creative coloring and drawing) and 50 percent copy work helps in learning basics.

If the child has trouble holding the crayon or pencil and just fists it, let him start off fisting it, and gradually he will get control over his hands and fingers. An older child (past the age of three and a half or four) who is still fisting the pencil or crayon might need the help of an occupational therapist to learn how to grasp it in a way that gives him more flexibility.

If children do these exercises effortlessly, you can go on to making complicated shapes, perhaps making a man out of a diamond, circles, squares, and rectangles—a little robot man, for example—with endless fun variations.

Motor Planning and Sequencing

After the first cornerstone skills—body awareness, balance, and coordination—are mastered, you can move on to activities in which the child has to sequence or plan many actions in a row. This involves, initially, planning movement starting with simple one-step actions like banging a drum, progressing to two-step actions like grabbing a car and moving it in a particular direction, to three-step actions such as moving the car into a house, to four- and five-step actions in a pretend narrative: The child moves the car into the house and back out, then "drives" to the school and then to the grocery store, and so forth. Motor planning involves carrying out two or more actions in a row, up to ten- or twenty-step actions, as in a complicated dance step.

For many children, the process of planning and thinking about their actions in their minds (some consciously and some more intuitively) and then carrying them out is challenging. By fifteen months of age, most toddlers are capable of taking Mommy by the hand, walking toward a desirable treat, pointing to the treat they want, nodding, and giving Mommy a beaming smile after she gives them the treat. This requires taking many sequential actions and is part of the child's repertoire long before she can say, "Mommy, I love you. Go get me the brownie." We have no evidence that the child is actually thinking or using ideas, but we can see that there is pattern recognition and some sort of planning.

Simon Says or Copycat Games

Many of the simple motor exercises and rhythmic activities that we suggested for motor functioning can also be adapted to help with planning and sequencing.

- **Rhythmic Movement.** This can be marching or jumping or dancing together in step with music.

- **Simon Says.** This game can involve a series of actions, progressively getting more and more complicated. If the child is having difficulty with copying your actions, then first copy whatever the child is doing and do it rhythmically. Then see if the child will copy you: "Now do Mommy" or "Now do Daddy." Try to make it fun. From one-step actions, banging a car on the floor, go to two-step actions, moving the car toward the child and see if the child moves it toward you. Then try a three-step action: getting a chair, sitting on it, and then standing on it. Show the child how you are doing it. Start off with the child doing each component part one at a time, then add in another step, and then three steps, and so on.

As we mentioned, this can also be done with fine motor exercises, like drawing. Make little lines and then squiggly circles, then squares, rectangles, and triangles, and then different sequences of these, starting off with just one, then two, then three or four. See how many the child can remember without looking back at what you have drawn and what she is copying. Again, make this fun, perhaps with little prizes for doing it.

Treasure-Hunt Games

In these games, children can be given three types of directions they need to follow in order to find a desired object.

- **Showing Where to Look.** First, just show the child where to look: look in one place, then two places, and then three places, and the prize is in one of those three places, all while saying what you are doing while doing it. The child has to absorb what you are doing and saying and then copy your actions.

- **Verbal Clues.** Then do the treasure-hunt game using just verbal directions. "It could be anywhere in the room, and here is your clue—it may be in the basket, but if it isn't in the basket, it will be in Mommy's shoe [which she has taken off] or in Daddy's hat [in the far corner of the room]." See if the child can look in all three places with verbal sequencing. Then you can go up to four, five, six, or seven options. The clues could be upstairs or downstairs, so that would take the treasure hunt into the whole house or the backyard.

- **Visual Clues.** Then use visual clues in which you point to the different places the prize could be, first with one or two places, and the child can take a look. Then point to three, then four, five, six, and seven places, upstairs, downstairs, outside, and so on. Eventually, the visual clues can be pictures of where the prize could be. For older children who are more sophisticated, make a map to follow. You can then number the different options where they can look from 1 to 10 . You can set up a system where children can lose points if they look somewhere that is not marked, and they get to keep the prize if they follow the road map and check all the different places marked.

- **Verbal and Visual Clues Together.** Next, the children can graduate to where there are both visual or verbal clues depending on the step—for example, step 1 is a visual clue that leads them to step 2, a verbal clue, which leads them to step 3, and so forth.

Treasure-hunt games can be great fun while also offering practice in motor activity, sequencing, and planning.

Obstacle-Course Games

As part of treasure-hunt games, or independent of them, you can play obstacle-course games where in order to find a hidden object the child has to negotiate an obstacle course.

- **Simple Obstacle Course.** Create an obstacle course where the child has to go over things, under things, through tunnels, around things—requiring multistep actions. He may have to get a stool to get over something or stand on something to reach a shelf to get the next clue.

- **Increase the Complexity.** Add on increasingly complex planned actions that require the child to plan actions while following a verbal or a visual clue or both. She may have to figure out how to get from place A to place G through places B-C-D-E-F. Start slowly and move on to more complex courses, again going through, under, over, and around things, opening and closing objects, and the like.

- **Instill Creativity.** Because you want to instill creativity in planning, have the child create an obstacle course for you to negotiate. Make it a two-way street: The child designs a course that you have to negotiate, and then you design one the child has to carry out. Designing an obstacle course takes every bit as much planning as solving it does.

All these games enable a child to do many actions in a row. He is building a fundamental human ability to plan ahead, to take many steps in a row, to take steps toward a purposeful goal. All of this is part of good concentration and focus.

Road Maps and Timelines

Once they have built up motor planning and sequencing skills at the level of actions and movement, and then at the level of using ideas, children can begin planning out their days, making a visual diagram of what they want to do, tasks and chores, and when they want to do these things. A timeline of the day keeps children on task and on target and improves planning skills.

Motor System Games and Activities

Motor Functioning

- **Evolution Game:** Help the child move up the ladder with progressively more challenging activities, from slithering, crawling, and walking to running, skipping, hopping, and jumping to agility and rhythmic activities.

- **Modulation Game:** The child controls his level of activity—faster and then slower and then superslow and then super-superslow and then from super-superslow back up to fast.

- **Body Awareness Games:** These help create better awareness of different parts of the body and greater awareness of the child's left side and right side.

- **Balance and Coordination Games:** These are very important factors in focus and attention.

- **Fine Motor Exercises:** These hand and finger exercises encourage close focus and attention.

Motor Planning and Sequencing

- **Simon Says or Copycat Games:** Motor-related copycat games and rhythmic activities, like marching or dancing to music together, can start simply and increase in complexity.

- **Treasure-Hunt Games:** These can involve verbal or visual clues of increasing complexity to find a desired prize at the end.

- **Obstacle-Course Games:** In order to find a hidden object the child has to negotiate an obstacle course requiring multistep actions.

- **Road Maps and Timelines:** Children can make visual diagrams of what and when they want to do a certain activity, chore, and so forth during the day or throughout the week.

- **Higher Levels of Planning and Sequencing:** There are many different forms of higher-level planning and sequencing, from complex movements and actions to fine motor aspects, as in sculpting and drawing, to the visual and verbal planning in writing an essay or play or composing music.

Higher Levels of Planning and Sequencing

After children reach the fundamental levels of being able to plan and sequence their actions, they will need eventually to get to the advanced levels required in school.

Planning and sequencing are needed in carrying out homework assignments and composing an essay, for example. Organizing a research paper and planning an experiment require even more complex sequencing and planning.

Often, we see children who have good memories and do very well in the early grades of school when everything—the basic math facts or word recognition—can be pretty well mastered through memorization. These children can be good readers, as well. But when it comes to more advanced work, they begin to have difficulties. Sometimes this shows up in writing assignments, and at times it can be handled through the use of their strong memory skills. However, in high school and college, when the work is more demanding, these star students may cease to shine because they haven't mastered fundamental planning and sequencing skills. Other students who have these skills, but have weaker memories, may start shining in the later grades. It's not that their abilities have changed; it's that the rules governing what is required have changed. Thus, there is no substitute for strengthening this ability right at the beginning when children are first learning how to sequence their thoughts. Creative thinking is also important at an early stage.

Essay Writing. One way to help a child who has to write an essay for school is to have him create a visual diagram with little boxes, with a few words about what he wants to cover in each box, leading up to his main idea in a big box. Use little arrows down to boxes with the supporting points and then a box for the conclusion. Then see if he can write the essay using the visual design.

Creative Thinking. Creative thinking, whether in pretend play or in creating a drama or a story, involves many complex actions woven all together. The grand epic is very different from the simple soap opera. Enjoy your child's creations and always be curious about them. Encourage more and more ideas: "Gee, that is fascinating—any other thoughts?" If the child switches topics suddenly and you are confused, help the child be logical and stay focused: "Whoa! I'm lost here. You were telling me about these new magical creatures you wanted to create on the Internet, and now you are talking about a computer game. How do these connect?" The child might say, "Well, silly, the magical creatures are part of the new Internet game I'm creating called . . . " All of a sudden it all comes together because you have challenged your child to make sense and stay focused while being creative. Then you challenge him even further to give you more reasons that something makes sense, in complex ways. Then the child can progress to the higher levels of thinking, like gray-area and reflective thinking, which we discussed earlier.

Visual-Spatial Sequencing. The sequencing can occur verbally, as we have just illustrated with creative play, but it can also occur in the visual-spatial worlds, such as mathematical sequencing in understanding complex forms of algebra and calculus. It also occurs by learning to apply scientific and mathematical principles to new problems in which you have to take a logical approach. Being an artist or a sculptor involves planning and sequencing, too—how you are going to transfer the image that you created in your mind to paper or with sculpting materials. We will come back to this later when we cover visual-spatial thinking in a separate chapter.

Music. Music is another form of sequencing ideas—for example, in composing. Many children diagnosed with ADHD or ADD early in their lives are gifted musically. I've seen one such child compose symphonies. Higher levels of thinking all involve the sequencing of ideas. Planning a new dance involves thinking at a different level, visualizing how it is going to play out in combination with a musical score.

CHAPTER 5

Organizing and Attending to Sensations: Sensory Processing

Children with attention problems often have difficulty with processing sensations, like sights, touch, sounds, smells, and so on. They can miss or overreact to what they see or hear, such as different gestures, vocal intonations, and the like. These difficulties make it hard for them to differentiate between their own and other people's emotions and between someone's true intent and imagined intent.

In a later chapter we will look in more depth at how children make sense of what they see and hear and develop complex visual-spatial skills. Here, we are concerned with how children modulate their reactions to sensory stimuli and become flexible in what stimuli they can handle.

Some children with attention problems are overreactive to sensations and get distracted by every sound or sight or touch. Others are underreactive, so sounds or touch or visual input hardly register. These children tend to get lost in their own world. They may get absorbed in imagination, sometimes in brilliant and creative fantasy, but they have problems interacting with others. Some children can enjoy fantasy and also be interactive and have good relationships, but are not flexible enough to do so at the same time.

Other children who receive the ADHD label are sensory craving. They seek sounds, sight, and touch and seem to want more and more. These children are extremely active and want to move and jump and crash into people and things. They are fidgety at school and can't sit still. This pattern is often the most challenging for parents and educators and all those around the child. As we pointed out earlier, people have argued from an evolutionary perspective that this kind of action orientation was once adaptive. In modern society, this view holds, we are constraining the natural and appropriate activity level of children. However, in today's world, at work, in school, in sports, or the arts, it is necessary to be flexible, to be able to adapt to the situation at hand. Enterprising and creative people can structure their own activity level, but you have to be organized and in control to do that. There will always be an occasional need to sit and listen in a classroom or take in what someone else has to say, or learn from others, as well as times when initiative and intense effort and activity are essential. Even the most physically active or quietly reflective of us needs to be flexible in how we modulate our activity. The "Sensory Processing and Motor Abilities Questionnaire" at the end of the book will be helpful in understanding the child's unique sensory processing profile.

Self-Awareness

There are two basic abilities that help children modulate their response to sensations: self-awareness and flexibility. As children become more logical and their thinking grows more complex, they begin to be able to describe their own internal world. "I can't seem to slow down." "I tend to get scared by these loud sounds but not quiet ones." When children can think in this way, they can control themselves and their environment better and thus stay calm and attentive. A child can say, "I'm getting fidgety. I need to go outside and run" or even ask a teacher, "Can I walk around a little bit while I listen?" An understanding, flexible teacher might let such a child walk around in the back of the room while listening to the lecture.

Using these higher levels of thinking, an overreactive child or adult can sense that he is not going to learn as well in a busy, loud auditorium, or he may avoid rock-and-roll concerts or go out on the balcony during a noisy party for some alone time. A child who is self-aware may also be able to help his caregivers, parents, and occupational therapists identify the experiences that are calming for him. Often rhythmic activities, such as music, or firm hugs or squeezing one's own forearms or hands will help soften the overload. Sometimes jumping on a trampoline, swinging, and getting what we call "vestibular input," that is, sensations in the inner ear, may be calming. The child may have noticed this about himself, and now he can act on it to help maintain his focus and attention. From more simple requests, such as "Shhh, Mom" or "Tone it down," to more diplomatic and elaborate explanations, a child can, in a sense, create environments that are more regulating and calming, in which he can pay attention and focus more easily.

For underreactive children, becoming aware of their inattention may take time. When adults ask them, "Where have you been?" or "Didn't you hear the homework assignment?" these children need to recognize that they were lost in their own thoughts. A child who can know his own tendencies and say to himself "I've been daydreaming again" is on his way to becoming attentive at appropriate times.

Flexibility

Children with attention problems also need to become more flexible in the level of sensation they can tolerate. A sensory overreactive child needs to be able to deal with an ever-wider range of stimuli. Parents and caregivers can help the child do this by combining soothing activities like rhythmic movement with very, very gradual increases in sound or touch (different light touches on different parts of the body) or bright lights or colors, and so forth. Find an activity that the child experiences as very soothing and gradually add exposure to a wider range of stimuli. The more verbal the child is and the higher level of thinking he uses, the more he can cooperate in these ventures.

A sensory-craving child may need to be exposed to gradually decreasing levels of sensation, and helped to notice more subtle stimuli—soft colors, whispers, light massage, and so on.

Games for Self-Awareness and Flexibility

The Overreactive Child

For children who like to be active, begin by getting active with them and match their rhythm—running, jumping fast, yelling loud, even muttering under your breath or fidgeting when they do. Then get into a kind of dance, making a game out of it, going from the fast movements to the medium-fast ones and then slightly slower, and slightly slower, and slower until you are really in slow motion. All kinds of senses can be involved. Drums can be played from fast to slow to superslow to slow motion, or songs can be sung loud, soft, supersoft, super-supersoft, and bright lights can be dimmed, softer and softer. In all the ways you can imagine, in playing this game, the idea is to go from the 100-mph down to the 1-mph or the 1-foot-per-hour level. You play both the tortoise and the hare together.

By making a game like this, we in essence help children learn to enjoy regulating their own activity level. By recognizing their own patterns and turning their energy into regulating and modulating that activity—not giving up the high activity—they now can get it under conscious control.

A second strategy is to find a structured activity, such as sports, dance, and music, in which a high-level activity is needed at some moments and not others.

Drumming works better than other musical instruments for very active children because they can move their hands and legs while drumming and hearing the loud noise. They can also accommodate to the rules of drumming as they are doing this. Start off with a gentle touch with freelance drumming and gradually introduce some of the rules that create rhythms. Rhythms can be vigorous at first and then slower and then slower and slower.

Same thing with sports—you can begin by just running around haywire and then around a set of bases and then through different agility drills. A game of catch can just be informal and then follow rules, or be done while balancing on one leg or catching one-handed. You can make these games demanding and challenging while still keeping them fun. Over time (and this may take months or sometimes even years), the highly active, sensory-craving child can become a child who enjoys vigorous sports or dance or active games but can also operate very attentively and with full focus within the rules of those activities.

The Underreactive Child

For the underreactive child, you can begin by energizing up your voice as you gradually woo the child into more and more interaction. You'll need to have an extra-animated and extra-energetic voice to catch their attention. A useful strategy to encourage self-awareness is to pretend to be the one who is self-absorbed and lost in your own world. Let the child draw you out. Children who lapse into creative fantasy can learn to recognize this and become more responsive, paying attention to more signals from others. Such a child will do better with a teacher or instructor or caregiver who can generate a lot of energy of his or her own.

Orchestrating the Senses

In helping children overcome their sensory processing problems, an important goal is to help them use all their senses together—vision, hearing, and touch. We want children to get all the parts of the brain functioning together as a ballet troupe or a basketball team would. Just a game of throwing and catching balls and talking at the same time keeps many parts of the brain and mind working together. When you help an underreactive child learn a new dance step and demonstrate the movements in different areas of the room all while talking about the new step, you are helping him process bodily, visual, and verbal stimuli at the same time.

In summary, to help with processing and the sensory modulation, gradually focus initially on what is comforting and soothing for the child, or what is energizing, or what gives structure to the child's activity. In other words, focus on whatever the child seems to require and then go on to increasing his flexibility to tolerate and enjoy a wider range of stimuli. At the same time help him become aware of this ability so he can take charge of the way he processes sight, sound, movement, and so forth. With these principles in mind, you can help children become the masters of their unique biologies rather than being governed by them.

CHAPTER 6

The Role of Emotional Interaction and Thinking in Fostering Attention

In earlier books, such as *The First Idea* and *Building Healthy Minds*, we have discussed how children engage in increasingly complex emotional interactions as they progress up the developmental ladder. At each of the stages, progressively more complex emotional interactions lead to more advanced levels of thinking, language, and action. In this chapter, you will see how this emotional development contributes to greater emotional regulation and, thus, a greater ability to focus and attend. For this reason, work on the foundations for emotional and social interactions is an important strategy in working with ADHD. We will begin describing how this process begins and is fostered in infants and young children, and then how to foster it in older children and adolescents.

The Earliest Foundations for Attention, Engagement, and Focused Thinking

Before we describe this process and how each stage contributes to greater and greater capacity to pay attention, it may be useful to look at the chart below that describes the different stages and the signs that the stage has not been mastered.

Foundations for Attention, Engagement, and Focused Thinking	Early Signs of Risk
Shared attention and regulation (*begins at 0–3 months*) Calm interest in and purposeful responses to sights, sound, touch, movement, and other sensory experiences (e.g., looking, turning to sounds)	Lack of sustained attention to different sights or sounds
Engagement and relating (*begins at 2–5 months*) Growing expressions of intimacy and relatedness (e.g., a gleam in the eye and joyful smiles initiated and sustained)	No engagement or only fleeting expressions of joy, rather than robust, sustained engagement
Purposeful emotional interactions (*begins at 4–10 months*) A range of back-and-forth interactions, with emotional expressions, sounds, hand gestures, and the like used to convey intentions	No interactions or only brief back-and-forth interactions with little initiative (i.e., mostly responding)

Foundations for Attention, Engagement, and Focused Thinking	Early Signs of Risk
Emotional signaling and shared social problem solving (e.g., joint attention) (*begins at 10–18 months*) Many social and emotional interactions in a row used for problem solving (e.g., showing Dad a toy)	Inability to initiate and sustain many consecutive, back-and-forth social interactions or exchanges of emotional signals

Enhancing More Complex Thinking	Early Signs of Risk
Language and creating ideas (*begins at 18–30 months*) Meaningful use of words or phrases and interactive pretend play with caregivers or peers	No words, or rote use of words (e.g., mostly repeats what is heard)
Building bridges between ideas: logical thinking (*begins at 30–42 months*) Logical connections between meaningful ideas ("I want to go outside *because* I want to play")	No words, or memorized scripts, coupled with seemingly random, rather than logical, use of ideas
Abstract and reflective thinking (*begins at 5 years of age and continues to adolescence and adulthood*) The use of higher-level thinking skills, including giving multiple reasons for feelings or events, dealing with degrees of feelings or thoughts, reflecting on one's own and others' feelings and thoughts, and making inferences (drawing new, reasoned conclusions)	Thinking is rigid and concrete, lacking subtlety or nuance; lack of self-awareness

Shared Attention and Regulation

A baby's first task in becoming able to focus and attend is to remain calm and regulated and to coordinate sensation with actions. In the early days of life, emotions help infants to bring all of their senses together and integrate them with their motor system. When a one-month-old baby turns to look at her mother to find that wonderful voice saying, "You're my sweetheart," she is coordinating vision, hearing, and action—listening, looking, and searching—guided by her pleasure in hearing this loving voice. This pleasure fuels the baby's first attention to the external world and coordinates her senses with motor actions.

Parents quickly learn how to grab the attention of their baby. For example, if the baby is sensitive to loud sounds, they learn to use a more soothing voice. For an underreactive baby who doesn't register sounds or sights easily, the caregiver will need to use more animation and energy. Some babies respond more to visual cues and others are more sound oriented.

Engagement and Relating

At this second stage, the two to four month old is becoming pleasurably engaged with the human world, showing a preference for Mommy or Daddy or other caregivers over the inanimate world or to all other sensations. A big, beautiful smile tells parents that the baby is fully engaged with them. Caregivers encourage the child to attend to sights, sounds, smells, tastes, and movement patterns by helping her become calm and comforted by rocking patterns, by types of touch—gentle, firm, tickly, or more of a squeeze—and by the quality and tone of their voices. Sooner or later, they find the right formula for comforting and soothing their little guy or gal. If the baby is very fussy, maybe due to gas or other distress, it can be a little more challenging, and parents may seek help to find the right approach. Perhaps it involves walking with the baby or holding her with firm, gentle pressure. Various strategies can be worked out, but the baby comes to recognize the caregivers as the source of comfort and anticipates being soothed more and more, often searching them out in a room or getting "bright-eyed and bushy-tailed," so to speak, as the caregiver enters the room. Here is not only a source of nutrition and fun and play but a source of comfort as well.

Purposeful Emotional Interactions

Around eight months, there is a real back-and-forth communication, with the baby reaching, vocalizing, and smiling, and the parents responding back—we call this opening and closing circles of communication. Now, through his facial expressions, arm movements, leg movements, body posture, and different sounds that convey emotion, the baby is letting you know what he likes and doesn't like. He is learning to regulate his own environment—basically

telling you to "shush" or to liven up a little bit. By attending to the parent's responses, the baby is beginning to get
a sense that "I can make an impact on the world." A baby
can now create a more pleasurable environment for himself
through his influence on others.

Emotional Signaling and Shared Social Problem Solving

Between ten to twelve months and eighteen months, a
toddler can engage in a continuous exchange of emotional signals with different expressions and more complex gestures and what we call shared social problem
solving. She can direct a parent's attention to what she
wants, whether it is to be picked up, hugged, or helped to
retrieve a toy. To do this she uses a tone of voice and gestures and expressions, and the parent responds with her
voice, gestures, and expressions.

These developing skills increase a toddler's ability to
create a more comfortable environment for herself. If she
is feeling overloaded, she can now let a parent know this.
She might hold her hands over her ears, or put them on
Mommy's ears, or, even better, hold her hand over
Mommy's mouth as though to say "Quiet." Not all toddlers can do this. Some will just get overloaded and cry,
but even a simple anguished look is a signal to Mom or
Dad or other caregivers to tone it down. The child who
craves a lot of sensation may grab Dad by the hand for

roughhousing or racing around the room together or take out a ball and start rolling it to Dad. She can clearly signal that she wants action. Without these skills, a child might just start running around the room knocking into things and be given an early label of hyperactivity.

Enhancing Engagement, Communication, and Attention

The Active Child

Many of the games we spoke about in Chapter 4, such as "Modulation Games," give children a chance to give voice to their need for activity and action, while also learning to regulate, that is, to modulate down. Rather than random activity, active children can learn to engage with others and give structure to all their energy. Children who are sensory craving can enjoy a lot of activities, but these games help them channel their cravings into an interactive framework—in other words, playing with another child or parent.

The Underreactive Child

When a child seems self-absorbed the parent can take that as a signal to energize up. Sometimes such a child might offer a clue to initiate play. For instance, a child who is quietly pressing the buttons on the pop-up toy might look at a parent very gently and sheepishly as though to say, "Do you want to do it too?" A parent can pick up on the signal and get into a little game.

Not only are parents responding to the child's emotional signaling, helping to counterbalance the child's tendencies, but they are also strengthening the emotional bond that helps the child coordinate all his senses into focused activity. Warm emotions fuel the motor system to work harmoniously with the senses and create connections between all of the different areas of the mind and, we speculate, the different areas of the brain as well.

Emotions and Processing Difficulties

For the child who is very vocal and may be repeating some words already, it is easy to ignore any lack of visual-spatial skills they may have. For such children, you might take some toy or treat or something the toddler really loves and put it in a special place in the room with a little barrier in front of it. Then you can say, "Where is the truck?" and make a game out of it with an animated expression. Offer a hand to help the child so that he can proudly march over to the barrier and knock it down to get the toy. Then you can make the game a little more complex, putting three barriers around the room so that the child has to search behind all three to find out where their special toy or treat is hidden. In all of this, the child's desire for that special toy or treat strengthens his visual-spatial processing skills. The child who before would look in only one spot can now look in three or four spots around the room and develop a sense of the whole room. He's beginning to become a "big-picture" thinker with a visual map of his world. Many verbal children with excellent memories tend to have a limited focus and need help in visualizing a whole scene. Games that create strong motivation, with favorite objects or competition, can broaden their range of attention at this early stage.

Enhancing More Complex Thinking

Language and Ideas

As children learn to talk and use ideas, they become still more in control of their world and more secure. They feel more calm and collected, regardless of regulatory or sensory processing patterns. They can use words and ideas to express desires. They can use words to say "Swing, swing" to help them calm down, or to get Daddy to hold out his hands, or "Jump" to bring out the mattress or trampoline. The child can now ask for what he wants.

Pretend play is another way of expressing desires. A doll can be "scared" because there are loud noises like thunder. Children can show you by the way they stroke a teddy bear whether they like tickly touch or firm pressure.

A child who is nonverbal can use pictures to show you what he or a doll likes. By communicating in this way he feels empowered.

Logical Thinking

At the next stage, as the child gets closer to the ages of three to five years, he is combining ideas. When you ask, "Why do you want to go outside?" the child says, "Because I want to run." Or he can explain when you ask why he looks sad that his sister won't play with him. The child who is combining ideas and understands cause and effect, noticing that this action leads to that result, can express that with ideas: "Mommy, that's too loud!" or "Mommy, I don't like it when the children bang into me" (for the child who is oversensitive to touch or sound). The child who needs more movement or sensation may say, "Mommy, I can't sit still. I need to go outside and run."

Visual-Spatial Challenges. Logical thinking can also be developed in the visual-spatial realm. Help a child figure out how block designs work, how mirror images work. For example, show how two identical amounts of clay can be in the shape of a snake or a ball. See if the child thinks the long, thin piece is better than the round one. You can do the same thing with a tall, thin glass of water and a wide glass of water. In all of this the child is developing logical thought, strengthening processing abilities, and at the same time engaging in longer and more elaborate focused attention.

Underreactive Child. A child who is underreactive may invite you into her pretend play if you have been a good social partner before. She may prefer a quiet game, but if you feel she is talking to only herself, that's your signal to energize up and make the pretend more creative and interactive. Also, this child might avoid physical activity that requires a lot of motor output. You might need to entice her through playing dress-up as her favorite TV character. The favorite TV character can go on an adventure with Daddy that will require going on balance beams and standing on Koosh pads and doing all kinds of interesting things. The point is, now the child can actually say to you, "Daddy, I'm scared! I don't know if I can go over the water on the balance beam" (a make-believe bridge). Daddy says, "Oh, I'll be here to hold your hand. I'll be here to catch you, and I'll be your superhero friend." He then encourages the child to take a chance. The newly developed logical thinking can help children expand their abilities in other areas.

The verbal child can now tell you when she is frustrated or doesn't like something, and you can empathize with her. This helps as you slowly expose her to more and more sensory experiences that she may not enjoy initially. By making a fun game out of it with a lot of verbal interaction and reassurance, when she gets used to it she is going to find it more fun. Let the child express her concern or anxiety or fear or worries, and if you listen and bring it into the pretend play and are empathetic, the child will gradually master these worries and fears more and more, and become master of her own feelings. The key is not to push the child to inhibit the feeling but to express it in a comforting, secure environment with an empathetic caregiver. A child who can express her feelings and even learn to control them is less apt to try to escape them in wild, impulsive activity or by constantly changing the subject.

Multicausal and Gray-Area Thinking

As we go up the ladder of logical thinking we get into multicausal thinking (between ages four and six years) in which the child can give you many reasons that he is feeling overloaded or craving more action. Then we get into gray-area thinking (between ages seven and nine) where the child can deal with degrees of feeling. He can tell you just how much touch he wants—"Just a little firmer" or "A little harder here, Mommy" as you give him a foot massage. Or as you are swinging, "A little more, Daddy" or "A little less, Mommy." So he can really now regulate his sensory and motor worlds and fine-tune them, not just go for all-or-nothing: "Slow." "Fast." "Stop."

The sensory-craving child, the child who is on the move, can modulate more finely—a little bit faster, much faster. Now you can have a dialogue and discussion while you are doing it, and the child can tell you just how he feels: "This feels really exciting" or "This feels a little scary" or "This is boring."

You want to help the child strengthen his ability to do multicausal thinking, to give you many reasons for why he wants to do or have something. Ask him why he wants to go next door. He may answer, "Because I need fresh air." "Why do you need fresh air?" "Because I've been sitting in school all day. Anyway, they are playing baseball, and that's my favorite game." At the same time while you are asking him "Why?" you are looking at your child and listening to him intently. The child is focusing because he is interested in the topic, and you're picking up on his natural interests and encouraging him to think in more complex ways about them.

Reflective Thinking

As the child gets older, his reflective thinking becomes stronger and stronger. He can identify his desires more confidently. He can recognize when he is calm and relaxed, or intense and active. If he needs a lot of adventure and excitement, he can deliberately choose to get involved in sports, dance, and outdoor exploration. If he likes more quiet time by himself, he can read or draw or write. These are his decisions. You can support your child in the kinds of activities that help him become calm and regulated and engage his full focus and interests. The reflective child becomes your partner in telling you what he needs, why he needs it, and how it makes him feel.

Regression in Thinking Level

Of course, if the child's emotions are very intense, if he is really overwhelmed, like any adult he can regress and become a polarized thinker or go back to becoming impulsive, scattered, or withdrawn. It happens to the best of us. We all need to recognize high intensities of emotion or sudden shifts. Now, one hopes, a child will become reflective enough to notice his behavior and say, "Gee, I'm out of sorts today. What have I been eating? What have I been doing? What's going on that might be making me nervous?" He can notice that he has been staying up late and was exposed to a lot of loud noises for three days in a row and his system is getting overwhelmed.

Always expect regressions when there are intense changes in the child's sensory world as well as the emotional world, in his relationships. Each new level of emotional development and thinking gives the child greater and greater mastery of his behavior, including his level of attention and activity.

Encouraging Emotional Development and Thinking Skills

When helping children to progress through these levels of emotional development and thinking that make possible self-regulation, attention, and focus, there are certain key steps for caregivers to keep in mind.

1. Help all the senses and the motor system to work together in harmony. In any game or activity, try to have the child looking, listening, moving, doing, and sometimes even smelling and tasting.

2. Engage in long conversations, verbal and nonverbal. Few children with attentional problems are able to carry on a long conversation or exchange of emotional signals. Often, they just have fragmented conversations instead of ten- to fifteen-minute dialogues. Make sure that your conversations cover many different areas of the child's interests, raising real issues, like homework, sibling rivalry, TV habits, and special privileges.

3. Increase the range of emotions that the child can express and tolerate. Disappointment, frustration, and anger are some of the emotions that are difficult for children with attention problems and self-regulation. Some become daydreamers, staring out the window when the teacher asks a hard question—"spaced out." Others become active or aggressive or have meltdowns or tantrums. Often this is because they can't handle negative emotions. For others, it may be the complexity that overwhelms them or a fear of failure. Bringing these feelings to the surface during relaxed chats will help a child recognize and control them.

When you are talking with a child, pay attention to her facial expressions. The child's verbal expression is not as important as being able to experience the feeling. If the child is verbal, have her describe the feeling. Let her express the full range of feelings from sadness to excitement, disappointment to happiness, anger to joy. Do this gradually by taking advantage of emotions that may arise as part of a natural conversation. For example, chatting about a schoolmate who "always has the answers" may bring up frustration.

"Thinking About Tomorrow Game"

In this game, the adult and child together picture the next day and how they will feel in certain situations—happy and excited or angry or fearful and anxious—and how other people might feel. The child is the talker, and you are the Socratic teacher raising the issue. If the child needs help, use a little vignette from your own childhood: "I remember when I was a child, I used to get angry when . . . "The most important goal of this game is to help the child become a poet of his feelings with animation and body language and tone, as well as in words. We want to help the child recognize the feelings at a preverbal level, which will help him avoid putting negative feelings into action. "Thinking About Tomorrow" helps the child anticipate feelings and think of ways to deal with a particular situation other than acting out. This is especially difficult for children with attentional difficulties and self-regulation.

---

4. Follow the child's lead and interests. If a child wants to talk about baseball or dinosaurs and shows interest with interaction, engagement, emotional signaling, and so on, follow his lead. You can throw in other topics and help broaden the conversation once the child is engaged and motivated. The child's interest should be the starting point for the interaction, but it doesn't have to be the ending point. Gradually throw in different themes, building on the child's concerns and pleasures.

Even if the child's immediate interests are rather narrow and repetitive—for example, playing computer games—if you join her in them, you can encourage creativity. Throw in conflict and curveballs to expand the themes. Ask how the people who are being attacked in the game are feeling, or how the game might have turned out differently. What would she have the players do if a crisis arose during the game?

When a child is fantasizing, make sure the dialogue is logical and always makes sense. It can be imaginative, but it should be based on a logical sequence—the magical power works because of A, B, or C.

5. Challenge the child's logic and self-reflection. Children with attention problems tend to think in fragmented pieces rather than connecting all the dots. We described this earlier with sequencing abilities, but logic will be needed in all spheres of learning and work. When talking about homework, for example, the child may suddenly switch to talking about a favorite computer game. Challenge the child to make sense: "I'm confused. I thought you were telling me about homework, and now we're talking about that computer game." "Well, Mom, talking about math homework reminded me of the game because you have to count in the game, too." Challenge the child to connect his thought patterns together and explain the connections. Debates about school rules, penalties, fairness, or even bedtime hours can bring out the child's best logical thinking.

Encouraging Emotional Development and Thinking Skills

Five Goals

1. Help all the senses and the motor system to work together in harmony.

2. Engage in long verbal and nonverbal conversations.

3. Increase the range of emotions that the child can express and tolerate.

4. Follow the child's lead and interests.

5. Challenge the child's logic and self-reflection.

Logic also helps with reflective thinking. A child with attention problems may not be able to reflect on an earlier instance in light of a current one and say, for example, "I got through the other test okay. Why am I nervous about this one?" This ability will be needed in planning a schedule or evaluating the child's own work to make sure all the pieces are in place. You can promote this by asking for the child's opinions: "Is there anything missing in your essay?" "I don't know." "Well, how did you reach that conclusion?" Or you might ask, "How does your first paragraph relate to the others?" "I'm not sure." "How can you stay on your main point?" "Maybe

I can list all the points I want to make and put them in boxes and then put the boxes in order." As you can see, logical thinking, sequencing, and the ability to reflect on one's work are closely related skills that bear on a child's ability to keep focused and attentive in school and other pursuits.

CHAPTER 7

Making Sense of
Sights and Sounds

Many children with attentional challenges have underlying difficulties with organizing and making sense of what they see and hear. They may have trouble using their eyes to focus, recognize patterns, and see themselves in relation to their environment. They may find it hard to follow verbal directions. It may be hard for them simply to follow a physical object from left to right or up and down and, later, to move their eyes across the page to read (tracking). Remembering a sequence of words can be a problem. Visual processing involves judging distance, and, therefore, children with these problems may keep banging into other people or objects, particularly if they and the other individuals are moving. Problems with "big-picture thinking"—seeing both the trees and the forest as part of the same whole pattern—can sometimes show up later in difficulty with understanding the concepts of quantity and, therefore, in mathematical calculations.

When confused because of these visual or auditory processing problems, a child may become inattentive in a classroom, drifting off into fantasies or becoming distracted by another child or a bird chirping in the tree outside. The child may not be able to keep up and may appear distracted when there is a need to learn something by copying what others are doing or saying, such as a new sport or song.

Making sense out of what we see and hear is an important contributor to our ability to think. As we will show, it's involved in how we understand time and the physical world we live in, as well as many academic activities.

When children are inattentive because of these difficulties with making sense out of what they see and hear, it's important to approach this problem by building from the bottom up. This should always begin with an eye evaluation and a hearing test, and consultation with a specialist if problems are found. The "Sensory Processing and Motor Abilities Questionnaire" at the end of the book will also help reveal the child's individual profile.

The following sections describe how children develop the ability to organize and make sense out of what they see and hear, and how these foundations may be strengthened if they did not develop fully. We describe some of the games and exercises that can be used to help children strengthen these foundations. If the child is older than the child in the example, the reader can adapt the game or exercises to make it more sophisticated. Not every child will need extra help here, but for those who do, this can do much to improve attention and problem solving.

The Stages of Visual-Spatial Thinking

Building on the work of Harry Wachs (see "Further Reading"), we can lay out the developmental stages of visual-spatial thinking. From the beginning, vision helps us understand how our own bodies work, to understand how our bodies work in relationship to others and in relationship to our physical environment, and to make sense of our physical environment. For example, how does a baby know that a series of shapes—nose, mouth, ears, and eyes—equals a pattern that identifies a human face? Newborn babies can discriminate such basic patterns, so the human brain seems to be prewired for that ability. But we then need to learn to make sense of these patterns. How does that skill develop, and how can it be strengthened?

Attending to Sights

Let's start with the first stage—regulated attention and interest in the world—and how it translates into a visual-spatial framework. What "attention" means is simply taking in sights and sounds, so we want to strengthen that ability. For newborn babies, this simply means encouraging them to look at Mother's face and listen to her voice, but for older children who may often be distracted, we stimulate attention by putting them in vivid environments and encouraging them to look around and point out details that interest them.

Strengthening Activities. During a nature walk, for example, ask the child to describe everything he can see—the colors and shapes of the flowers, the trees, the animals, the landscape, and the sky. Road-trip games are great for this: How many different cars or street signs or churches can the child identify? Have a contest between several children: Who can spot certain things first? Treasure hunts and hide-and-seek encourage detailed attention. Other games or exercises for this stage include those developed by Reuven Feuerstein, a visual-spatial pioneer, in which children identify details and patterns in images of dots. In dealing with attention deficits, whatever we're doing with the child—going on the subway, going to a museum, or just shopping for groceries—is an opportunity to increase the range of things he sees, to help him notice all the details. (It's important to do that in the real world as much as possible, but you can also use pictures in books.)

For children who get overloaded by visual stimuli, though, you want to be sure to expose them to new sights in a modulated way so they can feel calm and soothed, being careful not to exceed the level they can tolerate. Bright lights or sunlight can overwhelm many children, as can bright colors—you wouldn't want to take such a child to a carnival, for example. Other children are underreactive to visual stimuli; they need the loud, bright colors because soft colors won't draw their attention.

Coordinating All the Senses. While strengthening the child's alertness to detail, we want to coordinate sight with the other senses. For the child who is very self-absorbed and doesn't tend to coordinate sight with sound or with her own movements, find something she's very interested in. For example, enjoying an ice cream cone involves keeping it upright, tasting it, maybe smelling it, and feeling its coolness on her tongue.

Engaging the Visual World

If children are to pay attention and remain calm and regulated, they need to invest what they see with emotional meaning. It's not just about noticing the red ball; it's about playing a game with Mommy that includes the red ball. Then the child associates seeing the red ball with the pleasure of playing with Mommy and will pay more attention to it. We want to combine the physical, inanimate world with the human world, using vision as a bridge between the two. A child building a model railroad with his father will care about each length of track, each coupling and station.

Strengthening Activities. There are many games in which caregivers—parents or a sibling or a therapist—elicit the child's interest and attention. With a young child, maybe you start off by simply putting a little teddy bear in your pocket, with its head sticking out, so the child, in trying to get the bear, is relating to you and the object at the same time. Then you can gradually make it more complicated: Hide the bear somewhere, or give it a horsey ride so that the child has to come after you to get a horsey ride with the bear. This creates a visual link between you and the object in which the child is already interested, and helps the child learn to track because he's following your movements—left to right, up and down, behind the chair and so forth.

Visual-Spatial Problem Solving

At this point, we want to help the child become aware of his body and other objects in space. We want to help him develop his motor planning and sequencing skills (as described in Chapter 4) because the motor system is needed for visual problem solving. If the child has severe motor problems, such as in cerebral palsy, motor tasks can be simple, such as just turning and looking or using tongue movements, but there will still be some movement by which the child can indicate his visual awareness of the environment.

When the child becomes aware of his body in space and his body in relationship to other people and objects, he becomes aware not just of the visual world but of the interaction between himself and others. In playing with others, he must anticipate and judge the distance he has to cover to get to others across the room. He's also getting the sense of time—how long it takes to get there— without even knowing the concept of seconds and minutes. Along with visual skills, the concepts of space and time are now forming experientially for the child.

Strengthening Activities. If a child has some motor planning challenges, but not severe motor problems, you can go through the motor exercises described earlier (such as the Evolution Game). Keep attaching some visual goal to the exercise. For example, the child might be squiggling or crawling on the floor to catch up with his sister who is playing a racehorse.

We want to keep expanding the range of objects, colors, shapes, and so forth that we use—in interaction with our own bodies—to interest the child. Caregivers can play hiding games with an object—holding a piece of candy in one hand, then hiding it somewhere on themselves so the child has to find it. Is it in Daddy's hand? In his pocket? Is he sitting on it so the child has to push Daddy off the couch and run after him to get it? This way the child learns to use vision in a highly flexible way, and begins to develop real visual-spatial problem-solving abilities. Balance and coordination exercises are also important to develop because they allow the child to get a sense of his own body in space and to move fluidly in relationship to other moving objects.

In these games, you want to help the child integrate the left and right sides of his body; you can do this by encouraging actions that require using the left hand and right hand together and using the left and right feet together—climbing, running, jumping, and complicated crawling. One of the best ways to work on visual tracking, which is necessary for reading and playing computer games, is to play throwing and catching games. You can entice the child into first just rolling the ball back and forth and then to his left and to his right. For a preverbal child, you can then hold the ball and say, "It's high" or "It's low" and, as the child is reaching for it, say, "It's next to this" or "It's behind that." Long before the child understands the words, he's getting the experience of the different dimensions of space that will later become more meaningful to him when he develops verbal language.

There's no end to the kinds of activities or games one can come up with in order to facilitate visual-spatial problem solving. The important thing is to have fun, while keeping the child invested in you and in all the details in the environment.

Stages of Auditory Processing

A child first learns to decode sounds, like distinguishing a *t* from a *p*. For example, when she hears "Be tracient" instead of "Be patient," she may get confused. A baby must learn to distinguish different sounds. Fortunately, as children's nervous systems grow they tend to be able to decode the different sounds in what they hear by hearing them in context and associating them in experience. Japanese children learn to distinguish different sounds than American children.

Later, a child learns to sequence these sounds and thus to understand whole words. Next come combinations of whole words, and a child can follow simple directions, like "Please open the door." The child then begins to form different answers to *w* questions (where, who, when, and what). Eventually, a child is able to answer a "why" question (between ages three and four years), which means he is beginning to comprehend more abstract questions, like "Why do you want to go to the store?" or "How do you feel about your friend Johnny who is sick today?" or "How do you feel about Grandma being in the hospital?"

However, even if children can understand this, they may not be able to deal with a sequence of concepts or directions. Inability to put what they are hearing in a linear, sequential pattern is a common problem we see in children with ADHD. Imagine that a teacher says, "I want you to do the first three problems on your math homework, then show them to me, and then if you've got them right, go ahead and do the next three, and so on." Some kids have no problem in following that sequence. For other children, it becomes a blurry quagmire of words strung together, and they get lost somewhere along this highway of directions, in a ditch, so to speak. This makes them appear inattentive and often to be inattentive, because they may tune out when they get overloaded.

When children get confused you can encourage them to raise a hand and say, "Run that by me again" or "Slow down and give it to me one step at a time." With mild sequencing problems, in learning a series of steps in a new dance, say, the instructor can break it down into individual steps and repeat each step until the child catches on.

In a third stage, a child can process what she hears into abstract concepts. If a teacher is talking about how a character in a book was feeling, this is an abstract concept, and if the child doesn't comprehend this, she may tune out and watch something out the window. More abstract concepts come up in math, such as fractions and long division. When a teacher gives an explanation, some kids can get it easily, but others have difficulty. A teacher who recognizes this can help the child by offering diagrams, charts, or other graphic aids rather than verbal explanations.

Coordinating Sight, Sound, and Other Senses

Exercises for strengthening visual and auditory skills can be combined into a game of hide-and-seek, for example, in which the child uses both sound and verbal cues: "Beep, beep! I'm over here, behind the desk!" You can also play games in which the child looks at a group of objects, and then has to identify them blindfolded, using touch— and the sound as they touch other objects, and smell and taste if appropriate—and describe what each object looks like. In this way, the child learns to construct a visual image from the evidence of the other senses.

With children who have visual impairments, we try to construct a visual-spatial world from sound and touch and the child's own movements. So the verbal child can describe what something would look like by touch and smell and taste and motion. She can figure out where things are in a room based on where the sounds are coming from, as well as by being helped to walk over and touch those objects. This gives her a visual-spatial map of an area. Similarly, a child who has a hearing impairment may be able to use visual signals as directions in a game and associate the sight of objects with tastes and smells. The idea is to create as much of a multisensory picture of the world as possible.

Functional Understanding of the World. During this problem-solving stage, children also develop a sense of what different things are used for. They begin to understand the functions of physical objects in terms of repeated actions, a pattern of behavior. So it's important to have many functional objects in a child's world—a comb, a hairbrush, a bell, a toy telephone, a music box, a truck, a car, a doll. The child begins to see that each object is used in a certain way. This pattern of use is eventually labeled a "doll" or a "telephone," but the child sees the pattern and understands the function of the object long before she can label it. Even a sixteen-month-old child will imitate adults on the phone, putting it to her ear and making noises; she understands that its function is to communicate.

In our games at this stage, we want to introduce imitation and use objects functionally. For instance, grooming is very interesting to kids. Daddy may be combing his hair, and the child has to find her own comb, so she can imitate Daddy. In other words, now we want the child to relate to objects according to their function as well as their colors or shapes or textures. Kids gravitate toward this naturally.

Words and Ideas

Once the child is looking and listening, touching and smelling, recognizing patterns and exploring the world with all her senses, she is ready to use words and ideas and combine them in different ways to solve problems. These abilities build on the foundations we've been describing.

From the beginning parents help children label and describe with words what they're already seeing and understanding. While experiencing themselves in relationship to other people, animals, and physical objects, they're associating words and word patterns, and distinguishing between one and another. These abilities depend on having a lot of interaction with the physical world and the interpersonal world, playing with others in a moving, dynamic dance.

When a child is playing tag, for instance, she is using both sides of her body, noticing distance, getting a sense of how long it takes to get somewhere, combining her experiences with her senses, and associating words and ideas with these experiences. On the other hand, if the child is overwhelmed because she's in a noisy or visually chaotic environment, or she's underwhelmed because she is not getting much stimulation, then this whole area of verbal development is not occurring properly. So interacting in a calm, regulated way is crucial.

Strengthening Activities. To strengthen visual-spatial and auditory processing abilities together, use labels and words for what the child sees and hears. On a walk, it's natural to identify what we see and hear—plants and animals, birds and wind sounds, and lights and sirens. An easily distracted child could be asked to describe buses and trains and cars and the sounds they make. The supermarket, which can be a huge challenge for a hyperactive or distractible child, is a good place to practice this. Hide-and-seek games can be full of verbal cues: "I'm in the closet, the one down the hall" or "I hear a noise behind the big couch."

In all these ways we're enhancing visual and auditory processing, while giving the child symbolic labels for how the physical world is organized. A child can get a sense of spatial dimensions and how to symbolize them, simply by playing the games all children play, but with plenty of description and labels. The child can form pictures in his mind of what "above," "beyond," "below," and so forth look like. She can also learn to follow a sequence of verbal cues.

Recognizing Higher-Level Patterns

The next step is to challenge the child to understand the relationships of objects in space. To develop big-picture thinking, a child needs to classify what she sees, to recognize larger patterns that are now symbolized.

Strengthening Activities. Blocks in different shapes and colors and construction sets are great for developing greater visual-spatial understanding. Try using the blocks in a competitive game: Who can make a blue star out of blocks? Who can make a three-story tower? Children might get engaged in arranging blocks into a "rainbow," or vying to be the first one to have one of every kind of block that's in the pile. These kinds of games are great for strengthening symbolic pattern recognition. As they require listening to directions and sequencing steps, they also help strengthen auditory processing.

Among the concepts a child needs to understand, an important one is that of conservation. For instance, three blocks stacked end to end have the same volume as three blocks stacked like a tower. The best way for the child to learn these concepts is by actually playing with the objects and experimenting with the physical world, so she can experience how physical space and weight and quantity and shape can all be transformed. As suggested earlier, you might ask the child to experiment with clay. Take two squares of clay that are exactly the same, roll one piece into a ball, divide the other piece to make two smaller balls, and then ask, "Which has more clay in it, the big ball or the two little balls?" and see if she can figure out that they're the same amount. You can also use a food that the child likes to eat—such as cookie dough—and make it into different shapes. The child will be invested in getting the one that's bigger. You can also do this with juice—pour the same amount into a long, thin glass and into a short, fat glass and ask her which glass has more juice.

Through these kinds of games, the child begins to realize that looks can be deceiving, and that she has to take a multidimensional approach to figuring out whether one quantity of something is more or less than another quantity. This understanding takes place over a long period of time; for older verbal children who haven't yet mastered these visual-spatial concepts, ask them, "So, what do you make of the fact that you started off with the two things that were the same, and now you're telling me there's more of one than the other? Are you a magician? How did you do that?" Then the child can go back and experiment again—pour the liquid back into the tall, thin container or the short, fat container, or put the blocks that are lined up like a train into the shape of a tower.

As children get the sense of quantity and the various dimensions of space, they are developing some of the formal systems, such as what we call "one-to-one correspondence," that is, that "three" equals those three blocks that are piling up. They also begin to understand that the shapes they're looking at, the lines and circles and half-circles, make letters—*a*'s, *b*'s, and *c*'s—and that these letters correspond to sounds, and then that these sounds can be blended together to make words. In this way, play and experiments with a variety of objects make a foundation for more formal academic activities that may challenge a child with ADHD.

Activities to Strengthen Comparative Thinking. To further strengthen a child's understanding of what he sees and hears, we can introduce more complex games. For example, Harry Wachs has developed a number of games in which he has children copy various designs from different perspectives (not as the designs look straight on to the child, but how they look in mirror image, or how they look upside-down—that is, from the perspective of the person sitting across the table). So the child has to understand the directions and transform what he sees, picturing the design from another perspective, rather than just copying it. Or you might have a child look at a picture of the front of a house, and then draw what the back of the house might look like, and so forth. Then you can challenge the child to create his own design that he has to replicate from different perspectives. These kinds of games develop comparative thinking in the spatial arena, just as it's developing in the verbal arena.

Games with clay can also strengthen what we call gray-area thinking. You can start simply, by lining up balls of clay from smaller to larger, but then shape one piece of clay into a rope form, one into a ball form, one into a square form, and so forth, and then despite the shapes the child has to remember which shape has the smaller mass, which has the slightly bigger mass, and which has the biggest mass. She is playing with sequences of visual images and putting them in various relationships to each other, in what Piaget called "seriation tasks." This helps the child to understand (later on) the idea of graphs and helps with mathematical reasoning.

To keep a child with attention problems engaged in these activities, before we start calling the process "multiplication" or "division" or even "addition" or "subtraction," it is important to use real objects the child values—food, trucks, fancy blocks, coins, and the like. Let him experience and understand addition, subtraction, multiplication, and division with these items, and then you can give the process the proper label and make it more systematic, and you can also show the child how to represent it with numbers. As we pointed out in the last chapter, first the process has to have emotional meaning. If the child is negotiating for a brownie or a truck from among several of different sizes, he's going to be very invested in picking the larger brownie or the bigger truck.

Symbolic Thinking in Words and Pictures

As children reach these higher developmental levels, they are also getting into more symbolic expression. In addition to expressing ideas verbally, by giving labels to the different spatial dimensions, they can also do it with pictures, as their motor control improves. They can actually draw pictures of people, relationships among people, or designs and diagrams showing how things work. They can also act out ideas through dance or drama. Many forms of expression can keep a child involved and focused more strongly than words.

As children first start to use letters and words, Pat Lindamood, in the Lindamood-Bell Learning Process (see "Resources"), likes to have children make the shape of a *c*, for example, with their whole bodies, and walk a *c* shape out on the floor. Children can then begin symbolizing words, such as the word *dog*, by walking or dancing the letters out, by writing the letters, by drawing a picture of a dog, by saying the word, by pretending to be a dog and running around and barking, and by creating a dog from blocks or Legos. So as children begin to symbolize their worlds, we want them to do it using all their skills and senses, not just using the words they see or hear. This makes the symbols (the ideas) more meaningful and helps children integrate more of their sensory and motor worlds.

Reflective Thinking

In understanding what we see and hear, we also reflect on it and make judgments according to our own or others' standards. A child playing the drums can decide whether he's keeping a rhythm. A child trying to design a house can evaluate his design with pictures of Buckminster Fuller's or Frank Lloyd Wright's designs. A child drawing buildings and designing rocket ships can think about how well they might work. In encouraging kids in various activities, we also want to make sure that their rationales make sense, that their ideas are logical, and help them evaluate and improve their own work. Such reflective thinking keeps a child on track and focused, and is particularly important for a child with ADHD.

Once a child is hooked on an activity of her own choice, there is no end to the focus and skill she can bring to it. A child's natural bursts of creativity are channeled and enhanced when a child can step back and evaluate her own work. Whether it is coming up with new soccer moves or dance steps, fixing engines, or painting, both imagination and reflective thinking are needed.

Visual and auditory processing abilities are a key part of helping children with ADD or ADHD attend to the challenges they will face in getting along with others and at school. To summarize, the key steps in developing these processing skills are, first, to invest all parts of their world with emotion, that is, to care about what they are seeing and hearing. Next, they need to integrate these and other senses. They need to learn about different spatial dimensions and create logical connections between objects in space and a logical sequence in what they hear. Much experience with physical objects and play with others lays the groundwork for symbolic thinking, such as the concept of conservation. This, in turn, develops the foundations for math, science, and reading comprehension. Children who learn to reflect on what they see and hear are able to remain focused, recognize distractions, and follow through on their goals and dreams.

CHAPTER 8

Building Self-Esteem in Children with ADHD and ADD

One of the biggest challenges in caring for children with attention problems or hyperactivity is to help them feel positive and good about themselves. Many such children, regardless of whether they have broader special needs or just limited attention, suffer from low self-esteem. They feel bad about themselves.

A good illustration is Mark, an eight-year-old boy who, when he was talking with me, said, "My brain doesn't work." I asked him what he meant by that, and he said, "Well, when the teacher is talking, I'm staring out the window, or my body just wants to move and I get up and I walk around the room or I talk to my friends." I said, "Well, what do you mean your body just sort of does it?" and he said, "It just sort of happens. It's like my brain doesn't work." I asked him how he felt about that, and he said, "Bad." "What do you mean by 'bad'?" "Well," he said, "I have a bad brain, and it's just bad." Then he gave a silly little grin, like part of him enjoyed being mischievous, but when I told him he was smiling about something, he wouldn't comment. He just ignored it and said, "I get into trouble a lot. Some of the kids make fun of me because I get into trouble. Even my friends sometimes make fun of me." I asked him how that made him feel, and he said, "That makes me feel bad." I empathized, pointing out that a lot of things made him feel bad. He gave another silly little grin and nodded in agreement. I asked him if there was anything that made him feel less bad, and he thought and thought and then said, "Well, one of the things I like is magic, and my mom and dad got me a magic box with some tricks in it for my last birthday, and I like doing that. If the trick works, I feel good. I can kind of trick people." I said, "How do they feel when you trick them?" He said, "They feel dumb!" I said, "So it's fun to make people feel dumb with your tricks?" and he grinned from ear to ear.

As I chatted with Mark and watched him interact with his parents, I could see that he could focus and attend in a supportive situation. He could engage with me and with his parents with warmth; he could show us things and solve problems in a social way. He also came up with a lot of ideas and at times could be creative and make up stories. In fact, at another point during the interview, Mark told me that when he got into trouble, he sometimes made up a story about why he did what he did. For instance, one time when he was poking the kid next to him, the teacher asked him why he was doing that, and he said, "'Because he was making fun of me, and he made up a story that I peed in my pants and that wasn't true.' I told the teacher all that." Then he looked down, and I asked him why he looked down. He said, "Well, I made all that up so the teacher wouldn't be mad at me." I said, "Boy, you have a good imagination! You can make things up pretty easily!" and he smiled. Mark clearly could be creative and use it for self-serving purposes.

Mark could be logical and answer "why" questions, and he could even do a little bit of what we call "comparative thinking." During the interview I asked if there were any other children who did the same things he did in class. "Well, there is one other boy who also always gets into trouble and has a bad brain." I said, "Well, who has the worse brain?" and he said, "Well, I think mine is worse." I asked him why, and he said, "Because I do more bad things. I get into more trouble." When I asked him how bad he felt, he could show me with his hands that he felt very, very bad, which showed that he could do some gray-area thinking as well.

When I asked Mark about other feelings, like what else did he feel along with the bad feelings, and gave him some examples, like happy, sad, and angry, he could talk a little about feeling sad, but he had a hard time talking about angry feelings or about feeling embarrassed or humiliated. Whenever those feelings came close to being described or I even brought them up, asking whether he ever felt that way, he changed the subject and talked about something he wanted for his next birthday or anything else: "Oh, did I tell you about this new video game?" He had a hard time talking about those kinds of feelings, which was obviously contributing to his low self-esteem.

Mark's Profile

In looking at Mark's processing profile, in addition to his social interactions and thinking skills, he was reactive to certain sensations—noises and different kinds of touch would get him hyperstimulated—but also very sensory craving. He liked to move, he liked to touch things, he liked to get into environments that stimulated him, and he craved the very sensations that overstimulated him.

Mark was pretty good verbally and was a good talker, but he had a hard time remembering five instructions in a row. I did a little exercise with him during the interview in which I asked him if he could go get a toy and put it in a drawer and then get another toy that was in the same drawer and bring it to me and then to his dad, but he couldn't remember the sequence. On obstacle courses he had a hard time with the sequencing, although he was active and considered an average athlete by his peers. His fine motor skills were a little sluggish, although he liked to draw. He liked to do magic tricks, but he had a hard time making his letters and shapes.

Mark's ability to balance—for example, walking on a balance beam—was also a little bit below age expectations, although it was not really bad. He had some relative strength there but not quite where we wanted it to be.

When it came to big-picture thinking, Mark tended to overfocus on one or two details. For example, when I asked him to search a whole room for something, he tended to look in one spot rather than taking into account the whole room and figuring out strategically where the object might be. So there were a number of processing areas where he was not quite as strong as he could be.

Family Dynamics

In talking with Mark's parents, it became clear that there were some family issues that needed attention as well. Dad tended to be very punitive and thought Mark was just being bad and doing all this stuff deliberately and tended to take a hard approach toward him. He had few interactions with him other than scolding or punishing him with time-outs. He didn't get angry or hit Mark, but his voice was gruff and he had a very negative attitude.

Mom tended to get overwhelmed. She was an anxious, caring person, but she worried when Mark got into trouble and was very embarrassed when she was called into school to talk to the teachers. Mark was not doing well in his studies—he was getting Cs and some Ds and often did not hand in his homework. They had three younger children—Mark was the oldest—and she felt, just as she put it, overloaded. She was also mad at her husband because she felt he was unsupportive. She also thought he was too harsh on Mark and worried that Mark might get depressed and become a delinquent adolescent and use drugs and alcohol.

This family pattern had characterized their relationship with Mark since he was little. It turns out that since he was a little baby, Mark had been very active and sensory craving as well as becoming overloaded easily. So our task was to help Mark feel better about himself while instituting a whole program to help him learn to pay attention a little bit better.

The first step in our approach was to help the parents support the program we were going to recommend, and encourage them to help Mark feel better about himself. In working with Dad, we talked about why he was feeling so punitive and angry toward Mark. After many discussions, it turned out that Dad had an older brother who was very active and intrusive and had often hit him when he was growing up. He felt his parents had never protected him. Dad was very worried that Mark would get out of control and be a "monster" like his older brother.

Once Mark's dad saw the connection in his mind between Mark and his older brother, I encouraged Mark and his dad to have some "hang-out time," or what we call Floortime, when Dad came home from work. On the weekends they could hang out more and do special projects together. Dad could get involved with Mark and his interest in magic. I encouraged him to follow Mark's interests, to set limits when needed to, but to establish a warm relationship with him first. Dad was able to recognize that his worries about Mark and the connection with his older brother were fueling a lot of the anger he had toward Mark, and this helped him relax and enjoy his son.

With Dad being more supportive, Mom was able to calm down and be a little less anxious. Also, I encouraged Mom and Dad to start getting off by themselves once a week, which they had stopped doing. They were able to rekindle their own relationship. I was able to help Mom prioritize her work with all four children and also get some help in the afternoons. They hired a big-brother mentor, a high school student, to help carry out some of the recommendations that I made for Mark. Since Mom was so worried about Mark's future, I helped her put this into words and see these worries in perspective. She talked about her dad, who had a period of alcoholism and had gotten into some trouble with the law, and she was obviously very worried that Mark may have inherited a "bad gene." Talking this through helped her calm down and relax a little bit. Giving her a lot of support, a little bit of insight into her own family, helping her structure her day, and getting a high school student to work with Mark's program in the afternoon all helped to ease her anxiety.

Mark's Program

With Mark, we instituted an ambitious program that we phased in gradually. We wanted to see if we could help him overcome his attentional difficulties and do it without medication. We would keep medication on the shelf to try at some later point if necessary. We focused on the areas where he needed work, and also on giving him confidence in his strengths.

Sequencing. As we saw earlier, Mark had trouble with carrying out complex directions. Working with his parents and with an occupational therapist, we designed treasure-hunt games with two-step directions and then three-step and then four-step verbal instructions. We gave him pictorial instructions with diagrams and maps to help him with his visual-spatial thinking as well. In these exercises, we let him succeed about 75 to 80 percent of the time so we didn't overload him. We built the challenges up gradually with two- or three-step directions in which he could be successful and then added on a fourth and a fifth step until he achieved a 75 to 80 percent success rate. Eventually, like an Indiana Jones character, he had to go through a complex course requiring planning, like getting three chairs or a board to put over the chairs to cross a pretend moat that he wasn't allowed to step into to reach the treasure. We got a lot of new fairly inexpensive magic tricks from the variety shop to use as prizes, so he was very motivated to pay attention.

Planning. Mark also liked to draw. To help him with things like getting his homework done and turning it in, each day we had him actually draw, not write out in words, a little map of what he was going to do that evening and what was due the next day. We arranged for his teenage helper or Mom to do that with him after school. He would make a diagram, showing some play-time and then some before-dinner work and some after-dinner work and what was due the next day, and he would check each activity off himself. He would add lit-tle drawings, or sometimes he would choose to use words—we let him decide. He did all this on a big black-board so that at the end of the day when he got all his checks done, he could erase it and put up a new list for the next day. Whenever Mom or Dad was worried that he wasn't getting his work done or wasn't going to hand it in on time, rather than nagging him, they would just say, "Let's go look at the board together" and "Oh, boy! You have a lot of check marks today! Is there anything else you need to do?" Mark enjoyed tracing his progress on the big board.

Balance and Coordination. We also noticed that Mark was, as I mentioned, having some trouble with balance, though he was pretty good at throwing, catching, skip-ping, hopping, and jumping. We made balance exercises part of his play with his mentor/big brother who would come over and sometimes do this with him and a friend. Mark was actually rather popular. Even though other kids made fun of him at times, he had many friends. The high school student, who was a good athlete, would have a balance beam and Koosh pads to use with Mark and a friend. Each took turns being the leader. Mark could do some of the things really easily, like just standing on a Koosh pad or standing on a balance beam. It was when they got into the more complex balance exercises—like throwing and catching a ball while standing on a balance beam or Koosh pad, and then talking while throwing and catching the ball, and then throwing and catching the ball with one hand while standing on a Koosh pad and talking and telling jokes, and so on—that Mark had some challenges. Eventually, we had him doing magic tricks while standing on a Koosh pad or balance beam. He enjoyed that thoroughly and got better with his balance and coordination.

Mark's program also included plenty of running, jumping, hopping, skipping, throwing, and catching kinds of games, too, just to reinforce things he already did reasonably well, as well as his sense of competence. Because Mark didn't have a lot of fundamental problems in motor coordination and he had good muscle tone, we didn't have to work on some of the more basic exercises that we outlined in earlier chapters.

Regulation Games. We also played many regulation games with Mark—going fast, slow, superslow; playing the drums loud, soft, supersoft. Also, we exposed him to different environments—just a little bit of noise and a little bit of commotion and a little bit of touching, then in groups with friends banging into him, then more and more stimulation until he learned to regulate himself and not overreact in those situations, not become overloaded. The Modulation Games—fast, slow, superslow; playing the drums; running fast, slow, then in superslow motion—were geared to deal with his sensory craving, the moments when he became impulsive and sped from 0–60 in two seconds. He learned to enjoy slow motion. All this occurred over a period of many months. As we were doing this, we often asked him how he felt, and he became more and more able to reflect on his feelings.

"Thinking About Tomorrow" Game. During hang-out times, both Mark's mentor and his parents simply talked with him about whatever was on his mind. They also did the "Thinking About Tomorrow" game in which he anticipated situations that would be hard, others that would be easy, and situations that he enjoyed and didn't enjoy, such as subjects he felt were hard. We asked what he routinely did when he had those feelings and how that made other people feel and what alternatives he had. He had to brainstorm and come up with the solutions himself. We explored feelings that were harder for him—angry feelings, humiliating feelings. We would ask, "Well, are there other feelings, times when you don't feel just sad or happy?" to get him to describe his feelings with a little more subtlety. We made suggestions like, "Do you ever get a little mad—just a teeny, teeny bit?" and he slowly

began acknowledging angry feelings and even feeling embarrassed at times or scared, which was hard for him to admit. He didn't like to talk about feeling scared. In these discussions with Mom, Dad, and the mentor, Mark expanded his range of feelings and his ability to reflect on them.

As his program continued, Mark began to feel differently about himself and his "bad brain." Perhaps most important, we found something that Mark was really good at, in which he felt his brain did well. His skill with magic tricks was evident and deepened as he made progress in other areas. As he learned to sequence better, to carry out a series of steps, he could do more complicated tricks. We worked on his fine motor skills by showing him card tricks that required being dexterous with his fingers, which he really enjoyed. His parents enrolled him in a magic class, where he met other kids who loved magic, too. Magic became his "claim to fame," and he even performed for his school class.

In talking with Mark over time, we helped him identify the feelings he felt in his body just before he was about to get fidgety and walk around the room or bug another child next to him or poke someone. So what he identified as "my brain made me do it" and "my brain is bad" became a description of feelings. By reflecting on these feelings, he gained more control. During our discussions, Mark's self-awareness kept strengthening. Eventually, the reasons for his little smirk in the first session became evident, as well as the pleasure he felt when his magic tricks left other people feeling baffled and "dumb." After about eight months in the program, now more skilled in describing his feelings, Mark could see that it was fun getting other people to feel like their brains didn't work right.

General Principles for Improving Self-Esteem

1. **Understand the reasons for the attention problems and begin addressing them.** Rather than addressing the symptoms such as distractibility or hyperactivity, work on the foundation skills such as motor skills, modulation, and self-awareness. Progress in these areas will help the child feel more in control and will be reflected in the child's approach to her difficulties.

2. **Work on family dynamics.** Some families support low self-esteem, and others support high self-esteem. Parents who are very anxious about their child may be harsh with her or may be afraid to set limits. Appropriate limits set in a supportive and constructive way are as important as praise and rewards. If parents feel overwhelmed, finding ways to ease up on workloads and stresses needs to come before adding the commitment of a program for the child. These steps need to be real and practical, such as sharing child care and housework more equitably, or hiring household

---

help or a high school or college-age mentor for the child. A chaotic or overstressed household cannot give a child with ADHD or ADD the calm and secure atmosphere she needs. (See Chapter 9.)

3. **Find a natural talent.** Next, and critically important, is the need to identify a child's strengths, a special skill around which the child can really rally her self-esteem. For one child it might be art; for another child it might be telling jokes, or storytelling. The talents can be as varied as chess, working with animals, rock climbing, music, bird watching, or dancing. Every child has something she can excel at, even if it is not traditional schoolwork or a traditional sports activity. It is important to be open-minded and find something that the child really enjoys. It is equally important that you don't give a child a false sense of self-esteem by overpraising her attempts to succeed, or pushing her into an activity that impresses others. That doesn't work at all. It needs to be something that the child chooses and feels great pleasure doing. From that comes genuine self-esteem.

4. **Build self-awareness.** Gradually help the child understand her strengths and weaknesses so that she can begin substituting a more accurate picture of herself for feelings of helplessness and guilt over unwanted behavior. Recognizing that feeling angry or embarrassed is normal and anticipating the situations that arouse such feelings help children gain mastery and confidence.

As Mark did these things, he came to identify the feelings in his body as being normal and natural. Instead of feeling overwhelmed by the tasks that were hard for him, he became able to identify what he did well, like math when he could concentrate and practice it. He had a little harder time with reading comprehension, but he learned to persevere. With a little more diligence and practice, as he identified things that he was good at and not so good at, what his dad was good at and not so good at, what his mom was good at and not so good at, he began to see that like everyone, there were things that "my brain is good at and not so good at."

Gradually, Mark began feeling better about himself, and these feelings spilled over into the areas in which he had to work harder. As his high school mentor worked with him on balance, throwing, catching, and kicking, Mark became a better soccer player on the neighborhood soccer team. He also enrolled in Little League baseball. He became a better student. These real accomplishments in turn made him feel even better about himself. Dad's more supportive approach and the work on his blackboard maps were also a big help. One day he told me, about a year after he started the program, "You know, my brain works better now. I can do more things." The whole family was functioning better. Mom was less anxious because she was feeling more positive about Mark, and Dad and Mark enjoyed doing special projects on the weekends. Mark was no longer identified as an ADHD kid by his teachers or by himself or by his family. He could calm down, focus, and attend, and, most important, he now saw himself in a competent and optimistic light.

CHAPTER 9

Family Patterns

Parents and caregivers of children with ADHD or ADD quite understandably find it difficult to cope with children who are constantly on the move, physically and mentally. Raising a child with attention problems can be very frustrating. Yet there is much that parents can do to create the kind of calm and supportive atmosphere that helps children engage and focus.

When a child pulls things off the shelves in a supermarket or runs around uncontrollably and others look on scornfully, the parents will feel anxious, angry, or embarrassed or all three. They may feel humiliation or fury at the child who is embarrassing them. Most of us in this situation would feel a strong visceral reaction.

Throwing More Fuel on the Fire

A very common reaction is to shout at the child to get him to stop. Yet the child who is out of control, running around, and overexcited may be acting that way because he is already overwhelmed by a noisy, crowded environment. A child who craves sensation may be running around and touching and grabbing everything because there are so many tempting sensory experiences in the supermarket or restaurant or toy store. The same child may be pushing other children to get in line first to go up the slide. If this happens a lot, the parents may despair at having a child who is "out of control." They may scold and get angry, adding to the turmoil. Afterward, they may feel deeply guilty and think, "Why haven't we been able to teach him how to behave?" In their eyes they have tried valiantly to try to teach the child to have control, but because of his biological makeup, it has been very, very hard to do.

When parents' response to the child's behavior is to put their feelings directly into action without a lot of forethought and counter the child's impulsive actions with their own impulsive actions, this can only escalate the situation. This doesn't mean we shouldn't set limits or let the child know that there are consequences when he pushes another child, or when he goes out of control in the supermarket—we certainly should. But the first step is always to calm the child down and help him become regulated again. To do this, we may need to help the child remove himself from the place that is leading to the frantic activity or aggression or disorganization. It may mean taking the child out of the supermarket and getting into the car, where the environment is calmer. At home, it may mean engaging in activities that are soothing for the child, like a rhythmic activity with music or some deep pressure applied to the back or the arms or the tummy—a little firm touching. Or it may mean engaging in a quiet game in which you can begin modulating the child's behavior by going from fast to medium activity and then to a slow and superslow pace. This can help the child get back into a pattern of regulation.

Once everything is calm, then you can talk to the child, if he is verbal, about what happened. If the child is nonverbal because of other special-needs conditions, you may have to be intuitive about what happened, or you may have to suggest choices or use pictures so that the child can help you identify how he felt. Try to figure out together with the child what happened, and then if the child has crossed the line—hit or pushed, for example, not just yelled out loud or screamed—you want to let the child know there are consequences. There may be a time-out, missing or interrupting a favorite activity. Then the child can learn that when he is feeling overstimulated or losing control, he can tug at your arm to indicate he needs to leave the scene of the action. He can gradually become responsible for his actions. This may take many months or even years to accomplish, but it is an important and worthwhile goal. The principle here is to counterbalance the child's loss of control with calm words and gestures and help the child reorganize and regain focus and attention.

All-or-Nothing, Polarized Thinking

A second common reaction that we all have as parents (and I have three children of my own, so I can testify from experience) is to get locked into polarized thinking. We blame the child and label the child in our minds, even if not consciously, or verbally. If we don't think it is appropriate to say this out loud, we think, "Johnnie is bad, and he is being bad deliberately" or "He's got ADHD and can't help it." We get locked into that mind-set. This constricts the compassion or the understanding we can show a child or the search for underlying causes such as sensory over- or underreactivity or processing difficulties. With such a mind-set, a parent does not see the child's better moments or strengths. Not infrequently, we see that children with attention problems have a much harder time in one type of environment than another. At home they are little angels, but when they come to the busy preschool they turn into hellions on wheels and cause a lot of trouble. In self-defense, a parent will think the child is all bad or excuse the behavior entirely and give the child no responsibility for his actions: "This is just the way he is, and he is not going to change. He was born this way, and I have to love him as he is."

Illogical Thinking

A third common defensive reaction that is very closely linked to the polarized response is to become involved in illogical thinking, making up reasons for the child's behavior, subscribing to a theory that relieves the parent of responsibility. For example, a parent may have seen a program on TV or read an article that talked about something odd in the water or food chain. Latching on to this issue, a parent can then attribute the child's behavior to that arbitrary factor and cling to it, even though there may be no evidence that it is affecting children in this way. Many parents of children with special needs of any kind are understandably anxious and so eager to search for a remedy that they can become fixed on a single explanation instead of looking at the complexity of factors. Rather than trying to help the child learn to set limits, focus, or calm down, or trying to improve family dynamics, parents may overfocus on a single cause, which could be food additives, the school environment, or even the content of TV shows the child watches.

Blaming the Other Adult

In addition to illogical or polarized thinking or lashing back at the child, another common response is to focus on another "culprit" in the family. Who does the child take after? Is it Daddy, Mommy, Grandma? When a child shows problems, it's very easy for the adults in the family to blame one another. Then we have additional family tension and conflict—sometimes a lot of arguing, even fighting.

Parents of children with special needs have a hard time hanging in there together and working out their problems. You'll frequently hear one spouse say that the other spouse is so preoccupied with the child who needs special care that they or the other children aren't getting any attention. Sometimes this is never expressed outright, but the underlying tension leads to more accusations and criticisms of one another. Fathers have confided in me that they feel unnurtured and unloved, but they haven't shared this with their wives. Instead, they criticize their wives for not being good-enough mothers. This is unfortunate because often the mother is trying valiantly and needs more support herself. She may confide in me that she feels unappreciated and criticized, which only adds to her burden. A mother can also make the father feel like the "bad daddy," that he's never doing enough: If only he were earning more money . . . If only he were home more with the children . . . If only he played better with the kids. So both parents feel micromanaged and criticized and unloved, and there is very little intimacy between the two of them. Neither of them deals with the concerns directly, and both take it out on each other.

We can have these same conflicts between two generations—grandparents and parents. Often, parents of an out-of-control child feel that their own parents blame the problems on their parenting. Single mothers or fathers may feel even more isolated. They may feel that their friends or their relatives don't understand the complexity of the problem.

As we said, these tensions and conflicts or different types of "acting out" on the part of the family members contribute further to the child's difficulties. Whatever form this takes, whether it's aggression, distractibility, or self-absorption, the child's problems will only become worse. In such an environment, it becomes more difficult to implement the type of comprehensive program we have been describing. An effective program requires the family to work together, working off the same page with a concerted approach. They can each have their different tasks and skills: Father can work on outdoor games and motor exercises, and Mother can work on sequencing and planning, or a grandparent can work on still others. Older siblings or other relatives can help. But everybody needs to be working together as part of a team, not as individuals in a disgruntled group who are criticizing one another or causing more tensions. It is all too easy for the child's problems to precipitate conflicts in the caregivers, which then cycles back, and a vicious cycle may start where a child's problems become worse and worse. Therefore, our approach is to work at all levels—at the caregiver-child level, at the family-dynamic level, and bringing professionals or part of the extended family into the pattern when appropriate and relevant.

Teachers

Before getting into some steps that parents and other caregivers can take, let me comment that the same dynamics I have described for families also confront educators. A teacher is very likely to feel like a caregiver or a parent. Other teachers can come into the room and say, "What's the matter? Why can't you keep your class under control?" If there are two or three children with ADHD- or ADD-type patterns in the class, it can very easily appear to others that this is a teacher who is not organizing her class well, who does not have her class under control. She may get a look or a comment from another teacher or the principal: "You need to be tougher. You need to show the children who is boss." The teacher can feel all the things that a parent feels and needs support in the same way. We have to help teachers do a good job for these children. The steps that we recommend for the family can help teachers as well.

Creating a Supportive Family Environment

Step Back and Take a Deep Breath

Whenever a child is exhibiting signs of ADHD, take a step back, take a deep breath, count to ten, and think about the situation from the child's point of view. Try to identify the child's regulatory sensory processing challenges that could be contributing to the behavior. What is this child like physically? Think about the child's history. Does the child have difficulty understanding words, or does she miss visual cues? Does the child get disorganized by noise or lights or crowds? Is the child oversensitive to certain stimuli or underreactive, or does she crave certain stimuli? Yes, there may be biological factors contributing to her difficulties, and not all these factors are changeable, in the short run at least, and some not in the long run. But most can be overcome, or at least the child can gradually learn to compensate for them effectively. Whether or not parents choose to seek help for their child, they need to understand her profile, her distinct way of approaching and reacting to the world.

Avoid "Simple" Solutions

Complex problems often have complex solutions. The analogy of putting a child on an antibiotic for a strep throat doesn't work for most complex problems. It is very easy for families to turn quickly to medication—a pill that will solve the problem. It is not that medication shouldn't be considered as part of a comprehensive program, but it should never be considered alone or be the first thing you try. Once you begin a comprehensive program and see how the child is doing, you can then decide whether medication can or should play a role, and add it in later. I find that as a general rule, the less you are asking medication to do, the more likely it will be helpful if it is needed later on. As we have seen, often these challenges can be handled "without a pill" by strengthening all the child's processing abilities and her ways of coping with a tendency to get overloaded by different kinds of stimuli in the environment.

Work As a Team and
Bring Out the Best in Each Other

The third step is to make sure—and save time for this—the parents and other caregivers work together as a team. For parents, this means having regular time with each other in the evening not just to discuss the child but also to nurture one another. If they feel underappreciated and unloved, they will have a hard time summoning the patience and energy to meet the child's needs. A family will then tend to get locked into the patterns we have been describing. Parents need nurturing time as well as time to discuss problems with one another each and every day, often after the children are asleep. They also need at least one evening or other time during the week when they go off by themselves to keep that nurturing relationship kindled between them. If the caregivers are a grandmother and her daughter, they need to go off and just be together and enjoy each other. Nannies and sitters, of course, need both days off and appreciative support. Finally, there should also be regular meetings with the educators and therapists working with the child to coordinate an overall team approach. When families find they can't resolve all this on their own, they need to seek out a counselor or a therapist to help them try to resolve these conflicts.

Bringing out the best in the other means both support and self-awareness. For example, a mother can say to herself, "What kind of support can I give my husband that will help him respond less punitively and take a more compassionate and understanding approach to our son?" A father has to say the same thing: "What can I do to help my wife?" Both need to ask, "What does our child need, and who can best provide it? What makes me so irritated with him when my husband [wife] doesn't seem to notice? Why do I lash out so easily?" Each parent must take time to understand the other parent's feelings so that they can work together in a reflective way. A reflective attitude means being able to watch how you are responding and examine your own feelings and the feelings of your spouse, or in-laws, or parents, as well as the reactions of your child.

A reflective family sets more effective limits. Don't get caught up in trying to be consistently tough and a disciplinarian or easygoing and permissive. Thoughtful limits that don't overwhelm children help them eventually internalize limits and expand their own limit-setting ability.

The Supportive Family Environment

1. **Step Back and Take a Deep Breath.** Take time to understand what triggers the child's behavior and feelings.

2. **Don't Throw More Fuel on the Fire.** When a child is out of control, provide a calming response, one that helps the child reorganize and regain his focus and attention.

3. **Be Wary of "Simple" Solutions.** Don't accept a label for your child, or a single theory about a cause or cure.

4. **Don't Blame the Other Adult.** No one is to "blame" for the child's problems. Enlist the strengths of each member of the family, anyone who can help.

5. **Work As a Team.** Parents, caregivers, and teachers need time to meet, reflect on the hard work needed, and support one another.

6. **Find or Create Environments That Contribute to the Child's Growth.** Match the available educational or therapeutic settings to your child's particular profile. Provide a home environment that encourages calm engagement and progress up the developmental ladder toward reflective thinking.

Find Environments
That Contribute to the Child's Growth

Last, but not least, it is very important to find educational and therapeutic environments for the child that contribute to the child's growth. A busy classroom in a very busy school may be overwhelming for a sensory overreactive preschool or grade school child. This child may need a small, nurturing, soothing classroom and school atmosphere. You might have to search for a charter school or private school, or even consider home schooling if it is possible. You want to find an environment in which the child is likely to function at his best. (See also the next chapter on the physical environment.)

CHAPTER 10

The Role of
the Physical Environment

Perhaps the most controversial aspect of attention and hyperactivity problems in children is the role of the physical environment. This includes what the child eats (sugar, other foods, food additives, chemicals), exposure to airborne pollution, and light and sound stimuli. Does the physical environment have an important influence on the attention capacities of children, and are some children more sensitive than others? Before getting into specifics, let me share some general principles related to the controversies.

When there are competing or controversial results from studies looking at an issue as simple as whether sugar has an effect on attention, we have to consider the problem of subgroups. In other words, when you look at a large population or even a smaller group of thirty or forty children, you're usually mixing children with different profiles. They may share a common problem like inattentiveness or a high activity level, but may have different sensitivities. For example, one group of children may have a low threshold for excitement, and a little bit of extra adrenaline in their systems might cause them to be quite inattentive and active. But then there might be another group of children with a high threshold for excitement and containment, and the sugar might just give them a pleasant boost of energy that they enjoy and that actually helps them focus and attend even better. Similarly, a couple of cups of coffee will cause some adults to be jittery, while for others it just gets their day going. They may feel more organized and focused and more competent in what they do. It's the same with wine—two or three glasses of a fine red wine with dinner makes some people nice and relaxed and social, while it may get others a little tipsy to the point of stumbling or slurring their words, or they may become argumentative because they are very sensitive to the effects of alcohol. For still others, it may have no effect at all until they have their fifth drink.

There are also a lot of individual differences in the way people respond to different environmental factors. That is because everybody's nervous system is different. When the research looks inconsistent, it is often because we haven't considered the possible subgroups. Often, we haven't looked at subgroups because we haven't really known how to categorize them.

As we've shown in earlier chapters, we can divide groups of children based on their underlying ability to plan and sequence, to modulate sensations, to comprehend what they hear or see. We can look at children with one of these different profiles and see how they respond to elements in their physical environment. If we are going to resolve some of the controversies, as a general principle we need research that looks at subgroups in clinically meaningful ways, based on children's developmental profiles and patterns. If research studies treat all children who meet criteria for a certain problem on some questionnaire or some observational scale or test in the same way, we won't know what the results of these studies mean. Unfortunately, we are still in the Dark Ages when it comes to many of these questions.

First Steps

Be a Good Detective

Start off by investigating, looking for patterns. After a birthday party, for example, where your child has eaten all kinds of sweets and sugary things, how does she behave? When your child is in a very stimulating environment with a lot of noise and visual stimulation, how does she behave? When she is in a very dull, low-key environment with not much going on, how does she behave? This is your first step and will give you clues to things you may want to investigate more closely.

Get a Thorough Physical Examination. As part of a good pediatric evaluation, have the child's thyroid functioning (hypothyroidism can produce low energy and inattentiveness, and hyperthyroidism can produce a lot of activity and distractibility). Anemia can cause low energy levels, along with sluggishness and inattentiveness. A recent pediatric examination is very important to rule out any physical basis for the child's problems that can be corrected through proper medical treatment and management.

As part of the general pediatric evaluation it is also very important to rule out things like blood levels of lead and other toxic metals. These can be injurious to the child's overall health, affect attention and the way the child focuses, as well as affect the way the child is able to maintain a state of calm regulation, even in the face of a lot of stimulation.

Overall Nutritional Status. Next, look at the child's overall nutritional status. Does he have a reasonably healthy diet with a balance of proteins, fats, and carbohydrates, and plenty of vegetables and fruits? Many children don't have this type of balanced diet. Is the child getting proper vitamins and minerals in his diet or through supplements? A child who is not eating a balanced diet or isn't getting the proper vitamins and minerals can be subject to physiological challenges that will certainly contribute to behavior.

Aspects of the Physical Environment

What are the aspects of the physical environment that we need to take into account? Again, I want to underscore the importance of identifying and looking at subgroups. In the meantime, until the research is done, each family should look at their child as distinct and unique. He is the *n* of one (*n* meaning the number of subjects in the research being carried out). The key is to look at how your child, or a particular child if you are a caregiver or clinician, responds to his physical environment. Rather than starting with the working assumption of "Many children respond in this way to a noisy environment or a bright, highly lit environment or a crowded environment," ask yourself, "How does this child respond to this particular aspect of his physical environment?" Here are some aspects of the physical environment that we need to focus on and take into account.

Sugars and Processed Carbohydrates. Controversy surrounds the question of whether sugar can make children inattentive. Some studies have suggested sugar doesn't make children more inattentive or more active, and other studies published in respectable journals like the British journal *Lancet* have suggested that it can and does. There is a little-known study, for example, showing that glucose (sugar when it is metabolized) stirs epinephrine, or adrenaline, as it is more commonly known, in the body, and that certainly would give a person an energy boost. The question then becomes: Does this create more inattentiveness or increase the activity level in children? For some children it probably wouldn't, but for others it might.

What is the amount of sugar or processed carbohydrates in your child's diet? Processed carbohydrates, like white rice, as opposed to complex ones, like brown rice or other whole grains, convert quickly to glucose or sugar in the body, as do fruit juices compared to whole fruits, which take a little longer. Many vegetables take even longer. So foods that convert very quickly create a very quick glucose load for the body that some children may handle very easily, but it may throw children with a low threshold off balance. Also, it may stimulate some adrenaline release that may, in turn, stimulate increased activity or distractibility in some children. Again, look for a pattern for your individual child.

Additives, Preservatives, Colorings, and Dyes. The next area, again a very controversial one, is that of additives, preservatives, food colorings, and dyes. Some people believe these ingredients contribute to inattention and hyperactivity, and some people disagree. Here, too, I see a lot of individual variation among different children. For some children, red dye number 40 drives them wild as soon as they ingest something containing this dye. Some adults have this problem as well. For other children and adults, ingesting foods containing this dye has no effect on them at all. This doesn't happen only to children with

ADHD or ADD but may have to do with a particular sensitivity. It may not be a "food allergy" in the conventional sense of allergies. It may be a sensitivity, just like some individuals are sensitive to coffee or sensitive to wine, as mentioned before.

Here, too, you have to look not just at the load of artificial substances—chemicals in the diet—but you have to look at, in particular, what may affect your child. So additives, preservatives, food colorings, dyes, and anything that is not natural to the food, as well as particular foods—for some children, corn or eggs or dairy or gluten products—could be a culprit or cause a problem. Look for particular food groups as well as artificial substances that your child may be sensitive or allergic to.

There are more and more artificial substances being added to our food, including antibiotics added to feed to keep bacteria out of meat and poultry. There are hormones that are used to create more muscle in cattle. Any of these substances can be a problem for a child. Compare how your child does on an organic versus nonorganic diet and see if that makes a difference in the child's behavior.

When you are looking at these things, a useful way of doing your detective work is doing two weeks on and two weeks off a diet in which you have the child free of the substance you are checking for two weeks and then two weeks during which the child consumes products containing that particular substance. See if there is a difference in the child's behavior. Set up your own 1–10 scale on the behavior you are interested in tracking—the child's cooperativeness, ability to follow directions, ability to focus and attend and stay calm (assuming the family circumstances and the emotional triggers are the same and you are not going through a particularly rough time at home or the child is not having a particularly difficult time at school).

Airborne Chemicals and Toxins, or "Indoor Pollution." In addition to the chemicals in foods, a third aspect of the physical environment pertains to things that the child may be inhaling. What is in the atmosphere or in the air can also affect your child's behavior. These airborne substances get into the lungs and then into the bloodstream and are metabolized. Cleaning products, for example, and soaps, toothpaste, pesticides, paint, rug cleaners, or new products, such as rugs and mattresses, all have chemicals that can get into the atmosphere in your home or the school environment and affect a child's behavior. Clothing or bedding or upholstery with fire retardants can also affect a child. For example, a new carpet will have all kinds of chemicals at the level where a child might play, even though you may not notice it as much while standing in the room. If you just cleaned a carpet or just had your wood floors redone, you'll smell those chemicals. Many adults get headaches and a lot of children get more active if rooms of the house have just been painted. It can take a couple of months to fully air out the rooms. Oil-based paints take the longest, whereas latex-based paints take a shorter amount of time. There are special paints now that are nontoxic and air out in a day or two.

What you use to wash the children's clothes is another factor to watch. There are Web sites listed at the end of this book (see "Resources") that look at chemicals that can affect children's physical environments and how they can affect health. It is not only attention and hyperactivity that can be a problem, but also proneness to illness, including infectious disease and cancer. Parents would do well to look at these Web sites to learn what to watch for in the physical environment.

Perhaps the school has recently completed some construction, and the materials may be giving off a lot of toxic substances. Pesticides in and out of the home are a concern because children will play on the floor or in the grass. There is no question that products like pesticides have toxic substances in them because their purpose is to kill bugs and pests. There are alternatives to these pesticides. Remember, children are going to be playing closer to where these substances have been applied, and they have a smaller body with which to absorb toxins. These toxins tend to get into the fat tissue and stay there for some time.

As we pointed out, there is controversy around all these kinds of chemicals and substances because they don't cause problems for all children. Some children will handle them better than others. Some will experience a reaction when the house is painted or new carpeting is installed, but others may not have any reaction. The re-actions can range from lethargy, depressed moods, and inattention to hyperactivity and impulsiveness.

Light and Sound. Noise and lighting levels, and different types of lights, can also have a strong effect on children. A child who has been very sweet, attentive, focused, and regulated goes to preschool where he is in a large, noisy class with a lot of activity and a lot of visual and auditory stimulation. All of a sudden he becomes overly active and very, very distractible. Mom and Dad get reports about their child different from those they have ever heard be-fore. This change in behavior may be a reaction to the new physical environment—the noise level, the lighting level, the way children bump into each other.

It is important to look at the actual physical environ-ment where your child spends time. The child's classroom might be near the boiler room from which the child, who may be very sensitive to low-pitched noises, hears a low rumbling noise coming from the furnace. Or the child may be near an environment that has high-frequency or high-pitched noises, or the teacher may have a high-pitched tone of voice. These are all things that need to be looked at when being a good detective.

The key point is to look at the child's physical envi-ronment systematically. Stay up-to-date on new research and findings, but regard your child as an individual, as unique, and don't rely too heavily on statistics. If the child's pediatrician makes specific recommendations, ask him or her, "Has the research behind that recommendation looked at subgroups of children, or has it just looked at children in general?"

Checking Your Child's Physical Environment

1. Make sure your child is healthy physically with a good pediatric evaluation, including levels of lead and other toxic substances.

2. Watch the child's behavior in different environments, after different meals, in different lighting conditions.

3. Try putting the child on an organic diet so there aren't any additives, preservatives, food colorings, or dyes in his meals. Minimize processed carbohydrates and sugars and juices and go for the slowly absorbing complex carbohydrates and healthy proteins. See what difference these steps make in the child's behavior.

4. For substances in food that may be causing problems, try a two-weeks-on/two-weeks-off diet, with and without that substance.

5. If you feel you've identified a culprit, try removing the substance from the child's environment or removing the child from the place that causes trouble.

6. At school, compare how your child's level of sensory reactivity, whether he is over- or underreactive or craving, fits with his teacher's style, the lighting, and the noise level in the classroom.

As you investigate the child's physical environment, while creating an optimal learning and family environment, take time to see how he does. Give him a fair period to adjust. You may be surprised to see that over time you have a more regulated, attentive, and focused child. The effects of many of these aspects of a child's environment on his behavior are controversial, and you should take the attitude that what matters to you is the effect on your individual child. Watch for new research, but seek the measures that help your child. Be a good detective, considering all possibilities.

For more information, see the Healthy Child Web site (www.healthychild.org) and the Environmental Working Group Web site (www.ewg.org), as well as other Web sites listed in the "Resources" section at the end of the book.

CHAPTER 11

Adults with ADHD

The approach to ADHD that we have described in prior chapters can be applied to adults as well, from teenagers to adults of any age. Adults can be in a better position to help themselves because they can assess their strengths and weaknesses more easily than children can. Just as parents and therapists profile a child's strengths and weaknesses—basic motor functioning, sensory processing, levels of thinking, visual-spatial thinking, auditory processing, and sequencing—so can adults monitor these areas for themselves. For example, a forty-two year old can take stock of himself and say, "I've always been inattentive and fidget a lot. I don't follow through on my projects as well as I would like to, and I'm always getting distracted. I never figured out why, but maybe I have ADHD."

Adults who find that this may be their problem often consider whether they should ask for medication. One man who consulted me said that when he was a child his parents tried Ritalin with him, but he became irritable and was reluctant to try it again. He had been told there are other medications available now, but he was reluctant to try them because he tended to be very sensitive to medications and their side effects. This almost middle-aged individual wanted to know if there was a program that would help him learn to focus and pay attention without medication. He was able to follow the guidelines that we have been talking about in this book and take stock of his own abilities. He was then able to institute his own program, similar to the one recommended for children with attention problems.

One difference between adults and children in applying our program is the need to make the activities interesting for the adult. Whether you are doing a balance activity—standing on one leg and throwing and catching a ball, doing an activity for motor coordination in which you are trying to use the left and right parts of the body together, or doing a sequencing activity in which you have to follow five or six complex steps in a row—try to make it interesting, taking into account your age, your abilities, and what your general interests are. For example, an adult who loves dancing might want to use dance for some of the activities. An adult who loves sports might use different kinds of sports practice and explore what sport will help with balance, what sport will sharpen visual skills, and so forth.

A Young Adult with ADHD

A very interesting case for which I consulted might bring this adult experience alive. A young woman I'll call Susanna who was twenty-eight years old came to see me. I had helped her younger brother with "ADHD" years earlier before I had formalized the program that I've been describing. She was impressed with how well her brother was doing. Susanna felt she might also have ADHD because, as she described it, "I'm very distracted by almost anything that goes on—it keeps me from focusing, and now it is beginning to interfere with work." She had managed to finish college and had a job on Capitol Hill working in a senator's office. Susanna was a very creative person and a good writer, but was being criticized increasingly for not following through, not finishing tasks, or going from one thing to another. In discussing her problem with friends, she was told that she may have ADHD and ought to consider taking medication. Like the man I mentioned earlier, she became very concerned because her brother had reacted poorly to medication. One time, Susanna confessed to me that she took one of his pills to see what it would do, and she felt kind of irritable and hyper and understood why he didn't react to it well. She wanted to know if a program could be developed for her similar to the one that worked for her younger brother. She needed to learn to stay on task and follow through. Susanna knew what her strengths were; her analytical abilities and writing skills were excellent. As part of her role in the senator's office she wrote speeches and helped articulate policy positions on domestic and international issues.

What could we do for Susanna? As we reviewed her functioning, she identified a number of areas where she felt strong. It was evident that Susanna was gifted verbally and had a large vocabulary. She shared some poems and short stories she had written. Interestingly, both her poems and her short stories had a scattered quality to them—they went off in all directions. Although she said that was all part of the creative intent, I think she was also justifying a natural tendency to be distracted and unfocused.

Susanna also revealed that she has always been "clumsy." She had had a hard time learning how to ride a bicycle and didn't ride a two-wheeler until she was ten years old because balance was always hard for her. Learning sports was very difficult for her, as was learning to dance. She also didn't like high places, didn't like roller coasters or similar rides, tended to get overloaded easily at parties and noisy environments, and was easily distracted by any sort of sound. Susanna could be working and hear a whisper from across the room and would stop what she was doing and eavesdrop a little bit to see what was being talked about. A bright light coming through the window would easily distract her. At a light touch on her shoulder, she would startle. Susanna was clearly hypersensitive to all kinds of sensations.

Susanna had had a hard time with math and difficulty understanding how things operated in space. For example, when asked to describe her house from different angles she found it hard to do. I gave her a little task with blocks, constructing a design that was the mirror image of one that she was shown. This stymied her. When she read something and I asked her if she could picture the things she read, that was a very hard thing for her to do, as were a number of other visual-spatial tasks.

At the same time, Susanna was a creative and logical thinker and adept at the higher levels of thinking, like "comparative thinking" (comparing two government policies, for example) and gray-area thinking (able to tell you how much better one was than the other), and was clearly able to be reflective about her own weaknesses and strengths. However, when it came to applying these same levels of thinking to the things she saw, Susanna wasn't able to do complex visual-spatial thinking. For example, when she looked at different designs and was asked to describe how they were similar or different and explain why, Susanna just gave up. She said her thoughts just ran all over the place. So she became fragmented and couldn't be logical. Susanna couldn't connect her verbal abilities with making sense out of the world that she saw.

Susanna's Program

The kind of program that we set up for Susanna could be applied to a forty-two year old, a sixty year old, or even an eighty year old. The key is discovering each person's interests and passions and then using them as motivation to carry out the steps in a way that is enjoyable for her.

Motor Planning. To work on what she called her "clumsiness," we wanted to start with the Evolution Game—slithering first, then crawling, walking in a more coordinated way, then hopping, skipping, jumping, and doing some trampoline work. Susanna made these exercises into a workout routine with music. She had already been doing activities to music to keep fit and was following an exercise show on TV. She had some of the audio recordings from that show, which she used to get herself going in the mornings, so she could easily incorporate her new exercises, setting the Evolution Game to music, into her routine. She found this amusing and fun, and it helped get her started every day.

Gradually, we added more complex left-right movements and sequencing. Susanna was never a good dancer, but she loved to dance. So she tried to master new dance routines using DVDs that had both visual and auditory instruction on how to do the latest dances. That helped her learn to sequence—she could see it, and she could hear it. To further her sequencing abilities, she set up some simple obstacles and combined them with the Evolution Game. She had to crawl through hula hoops and furniture and climb over different barriers, all of which helped her coordinate her body.

When it came to balancing activities, Susanna liked the idea of standing on balance boards and moving to music. She then combined tossing a ball up in the air with standing on a balance board and doing it rhythmically with music. We worked that into her basic routine.

To help further with balance, Susanna also did some yoga work. She had tried yoga once or twice before but found it quite hard to do because the different postures required muscle tone that she really didn't have. Now she approached yoga with a renewed vigor, feeling that it was going to help her pay attention. She attended yoga classes and did routines at home along with her dancing. Susanna attended some dance classes, too, once she felt she wouldn't be "embarrassed" and had gotten to a certain level of competency. All these activities together improved her motor functioning.

Sensory Modulation. Susanna recognized that she was very overreactive to sounds and had a hard time staying focused and attentive in noisy environments. It was easy for her to become overwhelmed and overloaded. So she identified, with my help, the different frequencies of sound that bothered her—low-pitched sounds like grumbling, sounds of a heating system going on, and motorized sounds were the most distracting for her. High-pitched noises weren't pleasant to her either, but they weren't as distracting. Gradually, Susanna exposed herself to these distracting sounds as part of activities that were very calming and regulating, like listening to music and rhythmic activities. Susanna liked soft country-and-western music with a slow pace. She could expose herself to different sounds as part of this music or while doing yoga movements that relaxed her. This helped her get habituated to them. Gradually, while these sounds still bothered her, they bothered her less, and over time she was less distracted by them.

Visual-Spatial Thinking. As I mentioned before, it was hard for Susanna to picture her house from different angles or picture things she had read. She couldn't turn stories into visual images. When I asked Susanna to picture her boyfriend and her best friends in a certain place as though she had just taken a picture of them, she couldn't do it. Susanna read a descriptive paragraph, and I asked her to picture what she had just read. She would always say she saw a blur.

Working on this visual-spatial area was more difficult for Susanna. We worked with blocks and different block designs. We worked with quantity concepts (because she always had a hard time with math, even picturing "big" and "little" was not easy for her). We did exercises with water in different-shaped glasses, the same basic conservation tasks that kids do in school but that she had never quite fully mastered. We helped her make more and more sense of what she was seeing and develop a sense of quantity by doing these exercises. Finally, she "got it," as she put it. This was basically hard work on her part, and we couldn't figure out an appropriate activity that would make it fun for her. However, she enjoyed where the journey was leading her.

To further strengthen her visual-spatial ability, Susanna started doing two things. When she wrote short stories or poems, she treated them like screenplays or stage plays and tried to picture how each scenario was laid out. Starting out with one or two characters and very simple dramas, over a period of six to eight months she built up to the point where she could actually picture things that she had written. From there, she became able to picture things that she was reading.

To apply all this to the tasks of her life, each morning Susanna would draw on a chart what the sequence of her day was going to be. Using little stick figures, she mapped out her activities or plans in terms of things she had to accomplish at work, things she was going to do for leisure activities, things she was going to do with her boyfriend or girlfriends, and so on. Rather than write them out as she had always done (she had pen marks all over her hands because she wrote things down to remember them), we had her draw her tasks using simple stick figures. This way she had a visual road map and timeline of what she needed to accomplish in a given day. She would keep checking this road map throughout the day, every half hour or so. She could see where she was in the timeline and where she had gotten off course. From that, the goal was to help her internalize the timeline, to create an internal road map with activities so that she could picture her progress and mentally check off tasks or activities as she completed them. Over a period of about four months, she was gradually able to do this. She kept working back and forth between the things she would say to herself and the things she would picture. The picturing was the hard part, but it provided a more cohesive guide for her. Although she was very motivated to do all of this, she also required a fair amount of encouragement. Sometimes she slipped and went backward and gave up on it, but then came back and persevered.

As Susanna improved the visual-spatial part of her thinking, she found that she was a better abstract thinker in general. She always saw herself as a person who had an eye for detail. She retained this ability, but she also became a better big-picture thinker.

As I met with her, I encouraged Susanna always to ask the question, "How does this all fit together? How do you put all of this into one big picture?" Whether it was a policy paper or a speech she was working on, what was the overall goal? What were the subgoals? Even though she was always a good creative writer, she often had trouble keeping the overall goal in mind. Now, when Susanna had to do a paper, she actually created a visual design with boxes and arrows going from the main point to the supporting points and realized how important it was to see things, not just to have the words in mind.

Over about a year, Susanna gradually improved her ability to stay on task, to follow through, to solve problems, to be less distracted and more focused. Her overall thinking abilities and the quality of her relationships and her life also improved because she was less frazzled, less harried, less fragmented. Her emotions were less chaotic, too, because she could understand her own feelings better and not feel pulled "all over the place." Feeling more calm and engaged, she could now gain some perspective when she was upset with her boyfriend or her parents or with something at work. She could see how the different feelings she was having might be related to larger issues.

Susanna made a lot of progress and really mastered the problems that she came in with a year earlier. She is a very good example of how adults with attentional difficulties can adapt the approach that we take for children and make it work for them.

CHAPTER 12

How to Identify When Additional Therapy and Medication Are Needed

How do you know when to get help beyond what you are reading in this book? The answer is fairly simple. If you try the approaches outlined in this book over a six-month period of time and your child does not show gradual progress and improvement, then it's time to seek the help of a professional who can give you further suggestions. Depending on where you think the problem may be determines which professional you see. If the challenge is in making sense out of what you see and hear, seek professionals who specialize in that area—a developmental optometrist or a speech pathologist. If the child still has problems sequencing his actions and being coordinated, seek the help of an occupational therapist.

You may want to have a psychologist or psychiatrist over-
see these additional therapies. If medications are recommended to help a child focus his attention, have a
consultation with a very qualified child psychiatrist or
pediatrician who specializes in using medications of this
sort. In consulting with these physicians, ask about their
approach to trying medication and whether they encourage combining medication with a comprehensive
approach. Do they discuss the side effects as well as the
benefits of medication? If the child is put on medication,
all the detective work of watching the effect on the child
described in Chapter 10 will be important.

These specialists may help you figure out the missing
piece in your child's development. But first cover all the
bases discussed in this book, including attending to family patterns that are stressful or don't challenge the child
enough to master certain basic abilities. Enhancing the
child's overall development is the goal along with overcoming attention problems.

As these efforts can be time-consuming on top of a
busy life, you may want to have a high school or college
student come help with the physical coordination games,
modulation games, and the like. With some direction,
this time can be used in a fun way to help the child improve balance and coordination and sequencing skills,
while at the same time learning a particular sport or other
rhythmic activity, like dance.

The general answer is to seek additional consultation if there are other difficulties that need to be addressed in the child's program, such as vision problems, or if the child is not benefiting from the program after following it for six months or more.

Sensory Processing and
Motor Abilities Questionnaire

Sensory processing and motor abilities influence a child's emotional and cognitive development. As we have shown in earlier chapters, they also affect a child's ability to attend and focus. The "Sensory Processing and Motor Abilities Questionnaire" provides a series of questions that can help parents and professionals identify how their child is unique. It is a way of systematically constructing a profile of the child's individual differences. Some children are overreactive to touch, while others are underreactive. Some are overreactive to sound, while others hardly notice sound. Each of these differences provides important guidance in creating a program to help the child learn to pay attention, be calm, and advance his or her thinking capacities. A child who is already strong in figuring out what he hears may need more practice in figuring out what he sees. Whatever the child's differences, there are ways to work with that child to help create strengths where there are weaknesses and turn vulnerabilities into assets.

Please note that the standard for all these items is the ability to function at an age-appropriate level. If the category itself is above the age level expected for the child, please ignore that category and go to the next one. For example, sequencing ideas would be above the age expectations for a one-year-old child but not for a four-year-old child. Please circle the number that most closely applies to your child under each question.

1a. When hearing loud, low-pitched (e.g., motorized) or high-pitched (e.g., violins, piccolos) sounds or in a noisy environment (e.g., shopping mall, airport, or busy classroom), does the sound seem to . . .

① Overwhelm and cause your child to withdraw, get upset, or become aggressive.

②

③ Clearly bother your child, but can be dealt with for a short period of time.

④

⑤ Not bother your child, unless there is a huge amount of it or not enough of it.

⑥

⑦ Not bother your child at all

1b. Do you feel that your child craves and seeks out the type of sounds described above?

   ① Most of the time

   ②

   ③ Some of the time

   ④

   ⑤ Rarely

   ⑥

   ⑦ None of the time

2a. When in a visually stimulating environment (e.g., bright lights, a lot of colors, many people), do the sights seem to . . .

   ① Overwhelm and cause your child to withdraw, get upset, or become aggressive.

   ②

   ③ Clearly bother your child, but can be dealt with for a short period of time.

   ④

   ⑤ Not bother your child, unless there is a huge amount of it or not enough of it.

   ⑥

   ⑦ Not bother your child at all.

2b. Do you feel that your child craves and seeks out the type of sights described above?

① Most of the time
②
③ Some of the time
④
⑤ Rarely
⑥
⑦ None of the time

3a. When hugging or cuddling with your child, or even when wearing certain clothes, does the sensation of touch seem to . . .

① Overwhelm and cause your child to withdraw or become aggressive.
②
③ Clearly bother your child, but can be dealt with for a short period of time.
④
⑤ Not bother your child, unless there is a huge amount of it or not enough of it.
⑥
⑦ Not bother your child at all.

3b. Do you feel that your child craves and seeks out the type of touch described above?

   ① Most of the time
   ②
   ③ Some of the time
   ④
   ⑤ Rarely
   ⑥
   ⑦ None of the time

4a. Is your child very sensitive to pain so that any scrape or bang tends to be very uncomfortable and even a little scary?

   ① Most of the time
   ②
   ③ Some of the time
   ④
   ⑤ Rarely
   ⑥
   ⑦ None of the time

4b. Do you feel that your child craves or seeks out pain so that, for example, he or she looks for ways to bang into people or things or engage in other activities likely to bring pain?

    ① Most of the time
    ②
    ③ Some of the time
    ④
    ⑤ Rarely
    ⑥
    ⑦ None of the time

5a. When in an environment with odors or smells or where, for other reasons, the sense of smell is stimulated (e.g., strong perfumes or food odors), does the smell seem to . . .

    ① Overwhelm and cause your child to withdraw, get upset, or become aggressive.
    ②
    ③ Clearly bother your child, but can be dealt with for a short period of time.
    ④
    ⑤ Not bother your child, unless there is a huge amount of it or not enough of it.
    ⑥
    ⑦ Not bother your child at all.

5b. Do you feel that your child craves and seeks out the type of smells described above?

① Most of the time

②

③ Some of the time

④

⑤ Rarely

⑥

⑦ None of the time

6a. When exposed to strong or new tastes (e.g., new foods), does the taste seem to . . .

① Overwhelm and cause your child to withdraw, get upset, or become aggressive.

②

③ Clearly bother your child, but can be dealt with for a short period of time.

④

⑤ Not bother your child, unless there is a huge amount of it or not enough of it.

⑥

⑦ Not bother your child at all.

6b. Do you feel that your child craves and seeks out the types of tastes described above?

① Most of the time

②

③ Some of the time

④

⑤ Rarely

⑥

⑦ None of the time

7a. When your child is in a situation where there is constant motion (merry-go-round or swing set), does the motion seem to . . .

① Overwhelm and cause your child to withdraw or become aggressive.

②

③ Clearly bother your child, but can be dealt with for a short period of time.

④

⑤ Bother your child only some of the time.

⑥

⑦ Your child is comfortable with movement and motion unless it's something extreme and new.

7b. Do you feel that your child craves and seeks out the type of movement and motion described above?

① Most of the time

②

③ Some of the time

④

⑤ Rarely

⑥

⑦ None of the time

8. Can your child carry out a complex set of actions using gross motor activities in an age-appropriate manner (e.g., learning a new dance step or learning how to play a new sport or negotiating his way through an obstacle course)?

① None of the time

②

③ Rarely

④

⑤ Some of the time

⑥

⑦ Most of the time

9. Is your child able to perform fine motor tasks in an age-appropriate manner (e.g., relatively good at copying shapes, penmanship, or being able to draw pictures with many elements to them relatively quickly)?

① None of the time

②

③ Rarely

④

⑤ Some of the time

⑥

⑦ Most of the time

10. Is your child relatively strong for his or her age in sequencing ideas, as in spontaneously arguing a point of view logically and cohesively or constructing an essay where one point logically follows another point (instead of, for example, tending to jump around from one subject to another—intuitively and creatively perhaps—but with more difficulty keeping arguments tightly sequenced)?

① None of the time

②

③ Rarely

④

⑤ Some of the time

⑥

⑦ Most of the time

11. Is your child able to follow multistep verbal directions easily and effortlessly for his or her age—compared to other individuals in that age range—rather than having trouble when a teacher or instructor asks your child to do three or four things in a row?

① None of the time

②

③ Rarely

④

⑤ Some of the time

⑥

⑦ Most of the time

12. Does your child have a relatively easy time for his or her age, when hearing a lecture or story, in seeing the big picture—understanding the main point and how other points relate to the main point (rather than getting fascinated, perhaps, with some of the specifics and having a hard time understanding the overall point of view of the discussion)?

① None of the time

②

③ Rarely

④

⑤ Some of the time

⑥

⑦ Most of the time

13. Does your child tend to have a wide range of ideas appropriate for his or her age about any subject and be interested in a wide range of subjects? In other words, does your child go on and on, free-associating about almost any subject under the sun or have a rich and vivid imagination (instead of finding it hard to talk for more than a minute or two without having first studied the subject or having a more focused imagination, preferring the real world to the imaginative one)?

① None of the time
②
③ Rarely
④
⑤ Some of the time
⑥
⑦ Most of the time

14. When your child thinks about a family member, does he or she easily "picture" the person's face clearly and vividly in his or her mind (rather than thinking about that person's attributes only in words)?

① None of the time
②
③ Rarely
④
⑤ Some of the time
⑥
⑦ Most of the time

15. Can your child systematically search for lost or hidden objects and often find what's missing, or does your child have a hard time with a sense of direction?

   ① None of the time

   ②

   ③ Rarely

   ④

   ⑤ Some of the time

   ⑥

   ⑦ Most of the time

16. Does your child enjoy and is he or she relatively gifted at, for his or her age, broad, theoretical explorations (i.e., the big picture)?

   ① None of the time

   ②

   ③ Rarely

   ④

   ⑤ Some of the time

   ⑥

   ⑦ Most of the time

17. Does your child tend to focus on the specifics or details of a subject (i.e., is he very good with facts and subtle details)?

① None of the time
②
③ Rarely
④
⑤ Some of the time
⑥
⑦ Most of the time

Further Reading

Brazelton, T. B., and J. D. Sparrow. 2001. *Touchpoints: Three to Six.* Cambridge, MA: Da Capo Press.

_____. 2003. *Discipline: The Brazelton Way.* Cambridge, MA: Da Capo Press.

_____. 2006. *Touchpoints: Birth to Three.* 2d ed. Cambridge, MA: Da Capo Press.

Bundy, Alison, et al. 2002. *Sensory Integration: Theory and Practice.* Philadelphia: F. A. Davis.

Dennison, P. E., and G. E. Dennison. 1992. *Brain Gym: Simple Activities for Whole Brain Learning.* Ventura, CA: Edu-Kinesthetics.

Ferster, C. B., and B. F. Skinner. 1957. *Schedules of Reinforcement.* Englewood Cliffs, NJ: Prentice-Hall.

Feuerstein, R., L. H. Falik, R. S. Feuerstein, and Y. Rand. 2002. *The Dynamic Assessment of Cognitive Modifiability: The Learning Propensity Assessment Device— Theory, Instruments, and Techniques.* Jerusalem: ICELP Press.

Furth, H., and H. Wachs. 1975. *Thinking Goes to School: Piaget's Theory in Practice.* New York: Oxford University Press.

Greenspan, S. I. 1975. "A Consideration of Some Learning Variables in the Context of Psychoanalytic Theory: Toward a Psychoanalytic Learning Perspective." *Psychological Issues* 9, no. 1. Monograph 33. New York: International Universities Press.

Greenspan, S. I., and N. B. Lewis. 1999. *Building Healthy Minds: The Six Experiences That Create Intelligence and Emotional Growth in Babies and Young Children.* Cambridge, MA: Perseus Publishing.

Greenspan, S. I., and S. G. Shanker. 2004. *The First Idea: How Symbols, Language, and Intelligence Evolved in Early Primates and Humans.* Reading, MA: Perseus Books.

Kranowitz, C. S. 1998. *The Out-of-Sync Child: Recognizing and Coping with Sensory Integration Dysfunction.* New York: Perigee/Penguin.

———. 2003. *The Out-of-Sync Child Has Fun: Activities for Kids with Sensory Processing Disorders.* New York: Perigee/Putnam.

Landrigan, P., and H. Needleman. 2008. *Raising Healthy Children in a Toxic World.* Emmaus, PA: Rodale.

Resources

ADD Resources
www.addresources.org (this Web site offers a National
    ADHD Directory)
223 Tacoma Ave. South, #100
Tacoma, WA 98402

Attention Deficit Disorder Association (ADDA)
www.add.org
P.O. Box 7557
Wilmington, DE 19803-9997
800-939-1019

Center for Children's Health and the Environment
www.childenvironment.org
Mount Sinai Hospital
One Gustave Levy Place
P.O. Box 1057
New York, NY 10029-6574

For information about the effects of the physical
    environment see:
Environmental Working Group
www.ewg.org

Healthy Child
www.healthychild.org

Interdisciplinary Council on Developmental and
    Learning Disorders (ICDL)
www.icdl.com
4938 Hampden Lane, Suite 800
Bethesda, MD 20814
301-656-2667

For a listing of DIR/Floortime professionals:
www.icdl.com/usprograms/clinicians/index.shtml

Lindamood-Bell Learning Process
For information about the Lindamood-Bell system:
www.lindamoodbell.com

National Institute of Mental Health (NIMH)
www.nimh.gov

A twenty-eight-page downloadable guide to the diagnosis, causes, and treatment of ADHD is available at
www.nimh.gov/health/publications/attention-deficit-
hyperactivity-disorder.

Index

About the Authors

STANLEY I. GREENSPAN, M.D., is Clinical Professor of Psychiatry and Pediatrics at George Washington University Medical School and Chairman of the Interdisciplinary Council on Developmental and Learning Disorders. The world's foremost authority on clinical work with infants and young children, he is a founding president of Zero to Three: The National Center for Infants, Toddlers, and Families and a supervising child psychoanalyst at the Washington Psychoanalytic Institute. Dr. Greenspan is the author or editor of more than thirty books, translated into more than a dozen languages, including *Engaging Autism* (coauthored by Serena Wieder, Ph.D.), *The Growth of the Mind, Building Healthy Minds, The Challenging Child, The Child with Special Needs* (coauthored by Serena Wieder, Ph.D.), *Infancy and Early Childhood, Developmentally Based Psychotherapy*, and, together with T. Berry Brazelton, M.D., *The Irreducible Needs of Children.*

JACOB GREENSPAN is Codirector of the DIR Support Services Center, which serves special-needs children, including those with attention problems.